Praise fo

MW01075426

**If you own a business, you owe it to yourself to read this book and implement the simple, powerful concepts for growth.**

From his foundations at P&G to rolling out the blue mountains on Coors Light, Gerry has influenced millions of customers to buy. The Because Framework reveals how any business can stand out and close more sales by answering four core questions. *They Buy Your Because* shares secrets used by billion-dollar brands and makes those strategies accessible to everyone.

**JIM TAYLOR**, President, Sonic, America's Drive-In

**A terrific read with numerous examples illustrating key concepts. I couldn't put it down.**

Listening to customers isn't an event; it's a lifestyle of learning. The Because Framework will help you transform insights into what customers value and identify innovations you can create that your competitors simply can't or won't.

**KEN GRAY**, Former Corporate Director of Innovation, Caterpillar

**They Buy Your Because delivers a framework that can be used by everyone from the CEO to your front lines.**

Gerry and his Because Framework transformed our sales force and our company. He took what seemed unwieldy and condensed it into clear, focused messages that we put on the road with our customers. Gerry is a master at simplifying the complex and making it actionable.

**MIKE STILES**, CEO, R&D Leverage

The Because Framework will help you deliver a consistent message even across an entire franchise system like FASTSIGNS.

When Gerry keynoted the FASTSIGNs convention, he knocked it out of the park. He helped our franchisees understand what they need to do to grow their profitable sales volume and prosper. His book *They Buy Your Because* makes his Framework accessible to everyone with a step-by-step process to influence customers.

**CATHERINE MONSON**, CEO, Propelled Brands (FASTSIGNS)

This book is an indispensable guide for leaders seeking to leverage Gerry's wealth of experience building big brands.

Just as Gerry has done for some of our largest Great Clips franchisees when presenting to them in person, he once again hits the ball out of the park with *They Buy Your Because*. It provides practical, actionable insights that will help you better understand your customers, provide them with more value, and ultimately grow your business.

**ROB GOGGINS**, President, Great Clips, Inc.

Gerry O'Brion challenges you to think differently about what you do … and, importantly, how you do it.

I believe in the power of brands and the power of their Because. *They Buy Your Because* is full of important information for those who want to differentiate their companies in crowded spaces and who want to lead through favorable influence.

**JEFF SINELLI**, Founder and CEO, Which Wich Superior Sandwiches

**Fresh. Simple. Relevant. Powerful.**

Gerry O'Brion delivers a timely and critical framework for creating a clear and trusted message. The Because Framework shows how to garner trust, even with customers who don't know you yet. Everyone who wants to sell something needs this!

**DAVID HORSAGER, CEO, Trust Edge Leadership Institute**

**I would highly recommend this book for any executive who wants to take their business to the next level.**

Gerry's Because Framework provides executives with high-level practical content they can implement in their businesses. Having led the Chief Executive Network for the past twenty years, I know firsthand the importance of providing actionable value. Several of our members have implemented the Framework and have reported a significant increase in revenue.

**ROB GRABILL, President, Chief and Senior Executive Network**

**This book will be a game changer for businesses seeking marketing success.**

Finally. The strategies of Gerry O'Brion's seminars in book form. *They Buy Your Because* uses engaging, relatable examples to unravel the secrets of influencing customers, provides specifics on how to find your Becauses, and inspires innovative thinking. It is an absolute must-read for business owners and entrepreneurs looking to thrive in today's market.

**CASWELL HUFF, VP of Field Marketing, Spectrum Reach**

**Enjoy the book and the process!**

We have been using the Because Framework for several years. It works. Any time you define your Because, it allows the brain to connect the rational with the emotional, which increases your influence. Follow the Framework, ask the hard questions, and validate your assumptions. This process gets you out of your comfort zone. Do the work and you will find Becauses where you never thought to look.

**KEVIN SPELTZ**, President, Clipper Distributing Co.

**I highly recommend this book for any business interested in intentional growth.**

Gerry's Because Framework gave us a common language to talk about growing very different businesses. Now all our choices and activities must first pass through the filter of our Becauses.

**JOHNNY GREEN**, President, RPM Industrial Coatings Group

**This book is worth your time.**

Effectively communicating value proposition is a challenge for most businesses. Gerry is a master at simplifying it into easy-to-understand Because statements. Working with Gerry helped us create a common language across our global organization.

**ROBIN KILBRIDE**, President and CEO, Smithers-Oasis Company

**This is a message every executive should hear.**

Gerry's Because Framework will change how you think about your business, which will have a profound and lasting impact on your results!

**DAVID HICKS**, Former CEO, HomeVestors (We Buy Ugly Houses)

**It's a roadmap for innovation and influence.**

Any company and any industry can be disrupted. *They Buy Your Because* delivers a powerful framework of influence and innovation to change the game before someone else changes it for you. It's packed with case studies showing you how dozens of companies have used the Framework to change their trajectory of success.

**BOB ROBINSON SR.**, Founder and CEO, Kaivac

**They Buy Your Because has become a must-read not just for our staff, but also for our marketing committee and our board of directors.**

At the American Institute of Steel Construction, we've struggled to get people to embrace our message. With Gerry O'Brion's help, we created a series of Because factsheets that are resonating with our members and our audience—and, most importantly, are starting to impact the marketplace.

**SCOTT MELNICK**, SVP and Chief Storyteller,
American Institute of Steel Construction

**They Buy Your Because is an essential guide to standing out in crowded, competitive markets.**

We have implemented the Because Framework across all our business units, and each new acquisition learns the Framework. It has increased our focus as an organization. It has given us a consistent way to deliver our key messages and core values across every touchpoint, including marketing, hiring, and service delivery.

**GUS ANTOS**, Founder and CEO, Milestone Home Service Company

# CLOSING THE SALE
# IN A CROWDED MARKET

GERRY O'BRION

# THEY BUY YOUR BECAUSE

PAGE TWO

© 2023 by Gerry O'Brion

All rights reserved. No part of this book may be
reproduced, stored in a retrieval system or transmitted,
in any form or by any means, without the prior written
consent of the publisher, except in the case of brief
quotations embedded in reviews and articles.

Extracts from Kaivac.com on page 146 are
included with the permission of Kaivac, Inc.

Cataloguing in publication information is
available from Library and Archives Canada.
ISBN 978-1-77458-403-3 (paperback)
ISBN 978-1-77458-404-0 (ebook)

Page Two
pagetwo.com

Edited by James Harbeck
Cover design by Kendra Cagle and Page Two
Interior design by Page Two

The Because Framework™ is a pending trademark of Gerry O'Brion.
I Wish I Knew™ is a trademark of Gerry O'Brion.

TheyBuyYourBecause.com

*To Mom and Dad.*
*You taught me to walk and allowed*
*me to run when I was ready.*


*And to my goats.*
*Craig, Carl, Desmond, and Rally.*
*I love you little fellas.*

*Your opportunity as a leader is to initiate change that leaves things better than you found them. Your leadership can change your company, change people's lives, and change the world.*

*In order to change anything, you must be influential. You must influence others to follow you, to work for you, and to say yes to you vs. all their other options.*

*This book is for anyone who is ready to be a better listener, be a better leader, and build a better, more influential organization... that closes more sales.*

# Contents

# Preface

## Why Do People Buy This vs. That?

I N 2002 I started a new job in marketing at Coors Brewing Company. Two weeks after I started, there was a marketing department meeting at a hotel ten minutes from the office. I happened to leave for the meeting at the same time as the chief marketing officer. He turned to me and said, "Hey, Gerry! Why don't you ride over there with me?" I'm thinking, "Yeah! What a great opportunity to get to know the CMO." This man was my boss's boss's boss's boss—the head of all marketing for the $4 billion Coors Brewing Company. He had a long and successful career in beer sales and marketing. His level of success was clearly displayed in a brand-new, sleek Mercedes-Benz.

As I was getting into the car, it occurred to me that I should ask him something really smart... so I would seem smart. As we pulled away from Coors headquarters for the short drive, I thought through possible questions. I settled on what I thought was the most important beer marketing question of all. I asked, "Why does a consumer choose to buy one beer vs. another beer?"

I thought he was going to give me a ten-minute lesson about how customers choose and how we, as marketers, influence those choices. Instead, he said, "Well, if I knew the answer to that question, we'd all be rich!"

I looked around the beautiful car and thought, "Well, you appear to be rich. You're the head of marketing for a multi-billion-dollar beer company, and you don't know how we influence customers to buy?"

I spent the rest of my career uncovering the answer to one question: Why do people buy this vs. that, and how do we influence those choices?

This book is the culmination of that work.

I became an executive for multiple billion-dollar brands, and then a professional speaker who has delivered over one thousand presentations to tens of thousands of CEOs, sales professionals, franchisees, and marketers about how to influence customers to purchase.

During that time, I have implemented the Because Framework in industries as widely varied as HVAC, injection molds, software development, medical equipment, law, contracting, distribution, avionics, financial planning, banking, flower wholesaling, food processing, engineering, architecture, and many, many more.

In this book, I will tell you why customers buy—and how to influence them to buy from you.

# Introduction
## Create Your Becauses... Because

THIS BOOK is for people and companies that sell real things to real customers in competitive markets. We're not all Coca-Cola, Apple, or Harley-Davidson, and while many people write lots of things about those brands, *They Buy Your Because* is for the rest of us: companies and sales professionals who need to sell more this year than last, who need to stand out in the sea of sameness, and who need to close sales in crowded industries. This book is for those who need to land more new customers and get their current customers to buy more and bring more referrals.

*They Buy Your Because* reveals a framework of influence that will deliver results regardless of whether your business is B to B, B to C, professional services, a restaurant, or anything in between. You can put it to work if your company is large or small, well established or a startup.

I spent my career in marketing and strategy for big brands like Procter & Gamble, Coors Light, and Red Robin. I made

TV commercials that sold billions of dollars of soap, beer, and burgers. There is a technique that we use in commercials that influences you to buy, and you don't even know we're doing it. In this book, I'll reveal that technique and show you how to put it to work in your marketing and sales strategies.

**It's called your *Because*.**

The Because Framework includes seven steps and answers the question: *Why do people buy this vs. that, and how do we influence those choices?*

The Framework is the intersection of age-old advertising strategies and the science of decision-making, applied to today's toughest marketing and sales challenges. It draws from billion-dollar brand strategies, Harvard research, and Nobel laureate work on influence, but results in practical application. In this book, I combine my years as a corporate executive with over a decade of real-world experience implementing the Framework in companies around the globe.

When you finish this book, you will think differently about influence and how to use it in your business. You will see which messages, strategies, and innovations will be influential and which will not. You will know how to make your website, proposals, videos, and one-on-one sales conversations more compelling. You will close more sales, increase innovation, and drive referrals. You will view all advertising and marketing through a different lens. You will be able to see how others are influencing you. You will quickly be able to diagnose which marketing language is compelling and which sounds like fluff.

Companies are big collections of decisions. The executives, sales teams, and marketers who make the best decisions win. They grow over time. The rest eventually stagnate or fail. That's business. The Because Framework gives you a consistent methodology and language for debate, dialogue, and ultimately making the best decisions for your company. You can use the Framework to grow sales and margins, align your organization, drive referrals, create innovation, and deliver differentiation that's valuable to customers.

## We All Need to Influence Someone

You likely operate in a competitive market. The Because Framework of influence has been used thousands of times across hundreds of industries, each competitive in its own way. Whether you have three competitors or three hundred, you still need to be the number one choice to get the client, the customer, the project, or the gig. You need to be the number one choice to get the money.

You may need to close more sales. You may need to influence distributors or retailers to carry your product. You may need to influence donors to give money to your nonprofit. You may need to influence employees to work for your company. You may need to influence your leadership, executives, or board of directors to take your direction. You may need to influence your boss to promote you. Heck, you may just need to get your kids to put the bowls facedown in the dishwasher. We all need to influence someone. Regardless of who you're influencing, this framework will help you get your target to say yes to you.

The Framework is easy to understand, but it takes dedicated work to execute it well. Put it to work in your organization and it will help you create messages and innovations that close sales. I will demonstrate how to use the Framework effectively through numerous case studies, and I'll point out pitfalls to avoid. Everything you need to create powerful Becauses is right here in the book.

There are dozens of books out there on branding, marketing, sales, influence, decision-making, and brain science. They focus on many aspects of getting customers to buy, influencing people, creating a business plan, and understanding how our brain works. Some focus on inspiration and storytelling. Some focus on "tricks" of influence. Some are marketing frameworks. Some are written by PhDs who are deep in academia, some are written by storytellers, and some are written by "gurus."

This book is different from all those, because it delivers a simple, powerful, actionable framework that can be learned and used by everyone in your company from the C-suite to the front lines. It can profoundly change the trajectory of your success. It is for real businesses that sell real things to real customers.

Throughout the book, you will notice that I break from the flow to ask you questions from time to time. That is because my intention is not that you just read the book, but that you take action from what you read. The Framework and case studies are all structured so you are not simply learning, you are *doing*. To enhance your journey, videos and additional resources are available at **TheyBuyYourBecause.com.**

If you're already using a business-planning or operational process, the Because Framework will plug right into your system. If you're using a one-page plan (which you should be), the Because Framework will enhance all the planning you've already done. If you have an innovation process and pipeline, your Because work will make that process more impactful.

Your Becauses can be particularly valuable if you are not present when the purchase decision is being made and someone else is influencing on your behalf. This is also true if your company does not sell directly to your end customers. If you sell through a distribution network or retailers or if you're a franchise system, your Becauses will give clarity to everyone about what to say when you are not in the room.

Creating Becauses will align your organization, enhance your sales processes, and generate referrals. It will drive more valuable conversations, discussions, and debates with your team. It will turn you into a listening organization where ideas bubble up from the front lines and everywhere else in your company.

Your Because finishes your sentence of influence: "You should buy from us because..." It gives your customer's brain the proof they need to trust that you will deliver on your promise. It is the linchpin of influence. And most companies don't use it—or even know it exists.

# PART I

# THE FOUNDATION OF ALL BUSINESS

## Influencing Customers to Buy

# Why Would
# I Buy from You?

THE FOUNDATION of all business is one simple thing. You must get customers to give you money. That's it. Remarkable in its simplicity, yet exceedingly true. If you can do it, you have a business. If you can't, you don't.

There are thousands of things you need to do or delegate to run a successful business: operations, supply chain, accounting, hiring, coaching, real estate, insurance, finance, and everything else. But the foundation of business is *influencing customers to buy*. This precedes every other activity in business, and nothing else happens without it.

Once you make the sale, everything else is logistics. When the customer says yes, you go to work at what you know how to do. As complex and challenging as execution may be, it is a solvable problem. It's your business. It's why you do what you do. It is critical, and you know how to do it.

However, there are no simple solutions to attracting customers and closing the sale. Anyone who says there is, is probably selling you something. Getting a customer to say yes is messy. It's part art and part science. It's part emotion and part logic. And without it, execution never gets a chance.

This entire book is dedicated to you finishing this sentence: "A customer should buy from us *because...*"

Take out a piece of paper and write down your best ending to this sentence. Look at what you wrote. Read it out loud. Could any of your competitors say the same thing you wrote? If yes, you have not helped me choose you; you've just made me more confused.

Customers don't like to be confused. They want to make the right choice. They want to make a decision they can justify to themselves and to someone else—their spouse, their boss, the board of directors, their employees, their father-in-law, or their neighbor. Their decision is important, and they do not want to make a mistake. They want certainty.

## Customers Don't Buy: They Choose between Options

A while back, I was making ribs and realized I was out of barbecue sauce. I ran down to the grocery store to buy some sauce. When I arrived, there were forty-two kinds of barbecue sauce on the shelf. I went there to *buy*, but the activity was not buying: it was *choosing between options*.

To your customers, you look like barbecue sauce. And they're trying to figure out which barbecue sauce is right for them. Every day, your customers choose between buying from you, buying from your competitors, and not spending the money at all. They want to make the best decision they can with the information they have, as quickly and confidently as possible.

What does the label on *your* barbecue sauce say? What do your sales messages, proposals, website, videos, and one-on-one sales conversations say? If your label is the same as all the other labels, you have not given customers a reason to choose you; you have made them more confused. Again, customers don't want to be confused, they want certainty, and it is your job to deliver that certainty. If you are the same, you are quickly reduced to competing on price, and it's a race to the bottom.

Companies spend a lot of time, effort, and money to create marketing and sales language intended to sell their products and services. Often, the language sounds good, but it is ineffective. It doesn't influence customers to purchase because it puts the company into the sea of sameness.

Large decision or small, customers want to be smart, look smart, and make a good call. How people choose may seem complex, but their choices can be influenced with some very straightforward and powerful strategies.

## How Customers Decide

If you want to influence customers' decisions, you must first understand how they make them. So before diving into the Because Framework we are going to look at how decisions are made.

Every decision is partly rational and partly emotional. For hundreds of years, economists have assumed we make rational, logical decisions. When price goes up, demand goes down. When price goes down, demand goes up. That would be logical. But it's not that simple. We all know that sometimes we make emotional decisions.

For over one hundred years, marketers have been selling to your emotions. Buy our product and you will be more beautiful and happier and people will love you. Have you ever seen a TV commercial that made you laugh or cry? It made you emotional, but then you couldn't even remember what the ad was for? Emotion for the sake of emotion doesn't sell anything either. So what does?

Daniel Kahneman, the 2002 winner of the Nobel Prize in economics, is not an economist. He is a psychologist. He showed that we do make emotional decisions, but our brain, our gut, and our subconscious are looking for rational, logical proof that they are good decisions. He details his research in his book *Thinking, Fast and Slow*.[1] When we get buyer's remorse, it's because we made an emotional decision, and our brain cannot find a rational reason that it was a good call. I like to put it this way: your brain needs a *rational reason* to make an *emotional decision*.

## Your brain needs a rational reason to make an emotional decision.

We do make emotional decisions, but our brains are looking for *proof* that we are making a good call—proof that we can use to convince *someone else*. How often in your sales process are you influencing someone who then needs to influence someone else when you're not there? Your customer may need to influence their CEO, their board, or their spouse. They need to know exactly what to say on your behalf or you won't close the sale. The sea of sameness simply will not do. Your customer must know what to say to finish the sentence "We should buy from them because…"

## The Because Framework

The Because Framework has resonated with the tens of thousands of CEOs, business owners, executives, franchise owners, and sales teams in my audiences for three simple reasons: it is easy to understand, every company can use it, and it generates real results—it works.

The Because Framework has seven steps: four core questions, the "Core Four," and three action steps to optimize and deploy your Becauses.

### Core Four Questions

1. **Who are your ideal customers?** Narrow your focus. Be specific. Who are you perfect for? Who is perfect for you? Who are you influencing?

2. **What are your insights?** What do your customers want more of and less of? What do they hope for, and what do they fear? What problem are they solving? What are their preconceived beliefs?

3. **What is your outcome?** What's in it for them? What do you promise?

4. **What is your Because?** What's your proof?

### Three Action Steps

5. **Innovate.** Create new Becauses.

6. **Create your Because Platform.** Tie it all together—your insights become your outcomes, which are proven by your Becauses.

7. **Execute at every touchpoint.** Put your Becauses to work to close sales.

# The Because Framework

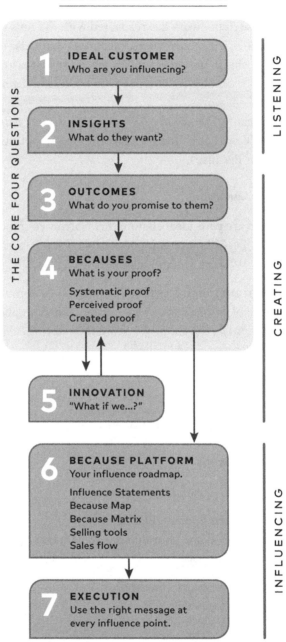

The visual on the previous page shows how the Framework flows. The seven steps start with the Core Four Questions. You begin by narrowing your focus and *listening* to your ideal customers, then progress to *creating* outcomes and Becauses. Creation continues as you innovate new Becauses, and then you move to *influencing* customers and closing sales.

## Competing in Crowded Markets

A few years ago, while traveling in Ghana, I visited a big open-air market called the Accra Arts Centre. It was filled with booths selling locally made goods. Most booths were selling basically the same things as other booths. Each vendor rented a space and displayed the goods they bought from the same local suppliers.

These booths were filled with wooden spoons, textiles, figurines, colorful bracelets, necklaces, and local clothing. The selection varied somewhat, but after looking at ten or twenty of the three hundred booths, I saw the exact same items again and again. It was truly a sea of sameness. It reminded me of the crowded, competitive markets where most companies operate.

Watching the vendors compete was interesting. Each booth worker had their own selling style: friendly, pushy, excited, bored, annoyed... Some were just sitting down in their chairs doing nothing. Some immediately wanted to be in a relationship. "Come in, come in, where you from? America, Canada, England? Have a look, have a look." Others cut right to the chase. "Good prices, good deal. Come on in, I have a special price for you." Again, a lot like in business: many different approaches, and some work better than others.

All the customers knew that the game was to find what they wanted and negotiate the best price. That's because almost everything was a commodity. Yes, the items were beautiful and locally made, but so were the things in the next booth. How do customers choose in a commoditized market? Price.

This example strips away all the complexity that many times clouds the foundation of business—we need to get customers to buy, or we'll go out of business. In a case like this, the fundamentals of success are quickly revealed. How can you create the smallest advantage? How do you make your booth more attractive? How do you build a fast, trusting relationship so the customer stops looking at the other booths? Does your booth location give you first access to the customers? These vendors compete every day in a tough, crowded business environment, just like you. Almost everyone in that market was negotiating on price for one simple reason: when all else is equal, customers will choose the lowest price.

I did buy several beautiful wooden spoons at a great price that day. I also bought one other thing. I bought it from an extraordinarily talented salesperson. Without knowing it, he used the framework presented in this book, and he did it artfully. Not only did he *not* negotiate on price, he didn't even have a booth—he was sitting on an overturned bucket. He was so good at influencing buyers that he had amassed over 200,000 views on YouTube—and they were posted by his buyers, not by him. His name was Mohamed Gungu.

Gungu understood *who* his customers were, leveraged *insights* about what they wanted, delivered an *outcome* based on those insights, and closed the sale using a powerful *Because*.

He understood that his customers were tourists. He knew what tourists wanted from items they would buy at the market. He understood their *insights*. He knew they wanted something locally made, packable, unique, interesting, with an experience—a story. They wanted something that would impress others or make a great gift. Those are the insights for international tourists shopping at a local artisan market. What are your insights about your customers?

Gungu delivered the *outcome* his customers were looking for, and he did it with a product that no one else was selling. He did not have the best location, the most attractive booth, or the best selection. He sold one thing, sold it well, and drew a crowd because he delivered on the insights of his customers. He provided the outcome they wanted in an engaging way that was hard for others to replicate. He sold a unique product and created a unique experience.

What did he sell? He sold an African music maker called a bakita, or asalato, made of two dried gourds on each end of a leather string. The gourds are filled with seeds so when you swing the gourds and they hit one another, they make a fun, musical sound. If you know how to do it, you can make happy rhythmic music with the gourds.

Sitting on a bucket, making these instruments, Gungu drew me in by making some music and then encouraging me to learn how to do it. He created the story and experience buyers were looking for from a small, packable, locally made, unique, and interesting item. He taught customers to make music, and as a result they told their friends about the gourds and about him. I bought a bakita *because* he taught me to play it, *because* it's a good story, *because* I can share it with others, *because* he made it himself, and *because* it's truly unique. He delivered on every insight in a powerful way. He was different from every other vendor.

I tried to negotiate price, not because the instrument was too expensive but because that is just what you do in that market. He simply replied, "No, the price is the price." His price cost me every remaining Ghanaian cedi I had in my pocket. It was worth every one. Gungu made *all else not equal*.

**At the end of the book, I include a matrix of every case study presented in the book.** It's a summary showing how dozens of companies have used insights, outcomes, and Becauses to create powerful language and messages to close more sales.

Visit **TheyBuyYourBecause.com** to view videos of Gungu and other videos mentioned in the book. You'll also find resources to help you find your Becauses.

## Valuable Differentiation Beats Price

All else equal, customers will choose the lowest price. It's your job to make all else not equal. The Because Framework is the art and science of making all else not equal. To attract customers, you need to be *different in a way that customers value.*

You need to be different in a way that convinces customers to vote for you with their money and their trust. If the things that make you unique are valuable to them, it changes the equation. That is the foundation of standing out in the sea of sameness, unique to you and valuable to them: *valuable differentiation.*

> ## All else equal, customers will choose the lowest price. It's your job to make all else not equal.

Whether you're in beer, air conditioners, architecture, or accounting, there are lots of choices for your customers. You need to help those customers cut through all the clutter and make the right choice—the choice to buy from you.

## Certainty Beats Relationships

Some executives say, "Marketing is great, but my business is built on relationships." Relationships are critically important for business and can be very valuable. They are formed through a track record of success; they build trust and they shortcut decision-making.

But what about new customers? How do you influence customers who don't have a relationship with you yet? How do you break through the clutter, get the meeting, and close the sale? Relationships are important but not sufficient.

### How do you influence customers who don't know you?

Would you say that you have a relationship with Amazon? Once I asked this to an audience and a woman in the front row raised her hand and said, "I have a relationship with Amazon... It's not a healthy one, but I have a relationship with Amazon."

I have a relationship with Amazon. I own a small hobby farm in Denver. I have four Nigerian Dwarf goats—Craig, Carl, Desmond, and Rally. The goats think it is very funny to escape from the pasture and eat everything in sight. I'm constantly fixing the fencing.

One day I ran to Home Depot to buy some welded wire fencing. I was standing in the aisle looking at the fencing and wishing it was a thinner gauge because it would be easier to staple. I pulled out my handy-dandy Amazon app and looked up welded wire fencing. Amazon had exactly the fencing I wanted and said it would be on my front doorstep in two days for less than the price of the fencing in the store. The reviews showed 4.8 stars from over two hundred people. I wouldn't even need to load it into my car. So, I clicked yes.

Yes, I have a relationship with Amazon. My relationship with Amazon was built in four ways. First, Amazon makes it exceedingly easy for me to do business with them. Just click and they take care of the rest. How do you make it easier for your customers to do business with you? What sticking point or barrier can you remove?

Second, Amazon communicates effectively with me all the way along my customer journey. From the time I place my order until it hits my doorstep, they stay in communication with me. I can even track the truck coming to my house. When it arrives, they take a picture of it at my door, and now Alexa lets me know that a package has arrived. I know exactly where I am in the journey every step of the way.

How do you stay in communication with your customers along their journey? Are you clear about what your customers want from your communication? Think about both the technology used to communicate as well as the timing and style of communication. How do you provide them with what they need, when they need it, and in a format that adds value before, during, and after the sale?

Third, and this is the important one, Amazon gives me *certainty* I am making a good decision. How do they do it? With customer reviews. The 4.8-star rating gives me confidence that I am making a good call. It's a powerful Because for Amazon. "I'm going to buy this one because... it has 4.8 stars." It gives me rational, logical proof that I am making a good call. Proof that I could use to convince someone else. We want to be certain that we are making a good choice, and Amazon gives us that certainty.

How do you give your customers certainty about their decision? What proof do you have that convinces them that they are not making a mistake? What proof can you give them that they will repeat to others?

Reviews are one way to create a Because. In Part III of this book there are seventeen Because creation strategies to help you create your own.

Finally, Amazon follows up after the sale. They ask for a review so that other customers know whether your experience with the product was good, bad, or otherwise. They encourage you to post pictures and videos of the product so other people are informed. They have you doing their marketing for them.

## Customers don't want a better relationship with you. They want a more valuable relationship.

How do you follow up after the sale? Amazon's follow-up helps them build their proof and gives them insights from their customers. Importantly, follow-up can also help you retain customers when something has gone wrong.

How can you make it easier for your customers to do business with you? How effective are you at communicating with them during your transaction? How do you make them certain they're making a good call? And how do you consistently gather customer insights?

Amazon has built a relationship with me, and I've almost never talked to anyone who works there except the drivers. Customers don't want a *better* relationship with you. They want a *more valuable* relationship. Relationships are important, but the nature of relationships in business is changing. Your relationship is great until a competitor comes along who gives them more value and a better Because. The time to figure out how to add more value is now, while you are still in the relationship.

Amazon has invested in innovations and improvements to methodically eliminate things that customers don't like and add things they do. They listen, learn, and innovate based on customer input. Don't like that you have to package and label your returns? Now you can just drop them off at Whole Foods—no label required. Don't like that it takes two days to get a delivery? Now you can get many items delivered on the same day you order them.

## Success with the Because Framework

Creating Becauses is the missing link to influence that many companies don't know about and most are not using. Your Becauses are the engine of the Framework, but it won't work to skip right to that chapter and begin there. The Framework builds upon itself, and every step is important. Listening sets you up for success; your Becauses finish the sentence of influence, "You should buy from us because…"; and then steps 5, 6, and 7 show you how to innovate and execute your Because Platform to close sales.

# PART II

# THE BECAUSE FRAMEWORK

## Four Questions for Influence

---

# Who Is Your
# Ideal Customer?

BOB ELERT was a certified auto mechanic who wanted to start his own repair shop. He leased a two-bay shop and called it 6th Avenue Auto. He had a huge sign made for the shop saying that he serviced two kinds of cars: "Imports and Domestics."

Yep, that's all of them.

He didn't narrow his focus because he wanted the biggest business possible.

When Bob opened, he thought everyone within three miles would get their car fixed at his shop because he existed. Not many people came in, so he did what a lot of business owners do: he started marketing. In his case, he placed door hangers on homes within three miles of the shop with a special offer for a $20 oil change. People flooded in for the $20 oil change—but not many came back.

Bob had a realization while doing the oil changes: lots of people in the neighborhood drove Audis and Volkswagens. So, he narrowed his focus. He changed his website to say, "Audi and Volkswagen Headquarters." He *specialized* in Audis and Volkswagens. I pointed out that his sign had a graphic of a car that was neither an Audi nor a Volkswagen. He was aware of that, but the sign was $2,000 and he couldn't afford a new sign, so he changed his website because it was free.

Narrowing your focus is one of the hardest decisions to make in business. It's uncomfortable. It's unnerving. It means that you might lose out on some business. Some businesses are convinced that they can serve all customers and serve them well. It is tempting to try to serve everyone, all the time. The problem is that spreading your focus far and wide slows your growth, complicates your business, reduces your effectiveness, reduces your efficiency, reduces trust, and reduces referrals. Customers want confidence that they're making a good call, and specificity increases that confidence.

The key is to convince each person you need to influence that you are the perfect choice for them and show them that you do something *unique* that is *valuable* to them. You must demonstrate that you understand them and their situation and are an expert in providing the solution they need. Your customers want and deserve someone who is specialized solving their problem.

When Bob changed his focus, people didn't start coming in from within three miles around. They started coming in from *all over the city*. Why? Now he had the real insight: there were lots of people who didn't want to pay to go to the dealer for their car repairs, but they did want to go to someone who *specialized* in their kind of car. Their car repair was important, and they trusted that a specialist would know how to do it right, for a better price than the dealer.

Bob tripled his business in eighteen months and within a couple years moved to a six-bay repair shop. He expanded his business by narrowing his focus. If you are clear who's perfect for you, they'll be clear that you're perfect for them. And when someone believes that you are perfect for them, they refer others who are like them.

## If you are clear who's perfect for you, they'll be clear that you're perfect for them.

Over and over, companies that focus more grow faster. This is not to say that you can't serve multiple customer types. You can. Most companies serve more than one type of customer. Some sell to different industries, some sell through distribution or retailers to their end user, some sell to different types of stakeholders during the sales process. The key is to make it clear to each of those customers that you do something unique and valuable for them.

Specialization shortcuts decision-making and increases trust. If you specialize in solving the exact kind of problem that I have, then I trust that you can solve it. If you don't specialize in anything, I don't believe that you can solve my problem as well as someone who does. And my problem is important; it's worthy of an expert. Specialization helps customers cut through the clutter. It gives people a reason to believe that you are the best solution for their problem.

Spend the time to determine who your ideal customers *are* and who they are *not*. Who do you serve the best? Who do you like to serve? Who do you *not* like or serve well?

Specificity speeds your growth because:

- It increases customer certainty.

- It increases trust.

- It increases referrals because people know exactly who to refer and what to say.

- It increases your prices and your margins. Customers are willing to pay more for a specialist.

- It reveals more actionable insights about your customers.

- It focuses your marketing.

- It focuses your innovation.

- It focuses your investment.

- It focuses your team.

- It helps eliminate low-margin customers.

- It increases efficiency and makes your business easier.

- It increases your expertise and effectiveness in your focus area.

## Identifying Your Ideal Customers

Identifying your ideal customers will narrow your customer universe—the total number of customers that you *could* sell to. That will help focus your marketing and sales plan, align your organization, eliminate work, and probably make you happier. The following list of questions will help you determine which customers are truly ideal.

You likely have an intuitive sense of the answers to these questions already. Ask your team these questions. Have them answer them from their own perspective. Analyze your customer and sales data. What do they tell you about which customers are ideal? Is there agreement throughout your organization about who your ideal customers are and who they are not?

1. Who is best served by you?

2. Who is least effectively served by your competitors?

3. Who is most enjoyable to work with?

4. Who is most likely to purchase?

5. Who spends the most per transaction?

6. Who is most profitable?

7. Who is most frequent?

8. Who is easiest to work with?

9. Who is easiest to find?

10. Who needs what you do best?

11. Who gives the most referral business?

12. Who is the best opportunity for long-term business?

Focusing is uncomfortable, but it's powerful. Do you have any customers that cause you more pain than they're worth? Many times, our least enjoyable customers also produce the lowest margins. But we keep working with them because we are not sure how we'll replace their revenue. Eliminate your low-value, low-margin customers who cause you pain and open yourself up to serve more of the customers who you love and who love you.

One pitfall that companies fall into when completing this exercise is describing their customers by dimensions that are not findable. They say things like "We want customers who believe in partnership" or "We want customers who understand the value we deliver." Well, yes, but how will you go about *finding* those customers? It's more valuable to focus on something specific that will help you identify and contact your prospects. Things like customers in a certain industry, of a certain size, or certain positions within your target companies.

The more you focus, the easier your customers are to find. How many potential customers are you selling to? Is your customer universe a hundred, a thousand, ten thousand, a hundred thousand, or millions? Understanding your universe simplifies everything else you do. It informs your entire plan. If you understand the size of your potential customer base, it becomes clear where to focus and where to put your messages.

If you have a hundred prospects, regardless of your industry, you can immediately come up with strategies to go after those customers. If it's a thousand, the strategies may be slightly different, and if it's a million, different altogether. Identifying your customer universe is a powerful way to lay the foundational strategies of your marketing and sales plan.

Over time, your best customers tend to present themselves. Do you have a segment of your company that is leading your growth? It's likely because those customers are clear on the unique value you are providing to them. They are certain they are making a good call. Salespeople tend to sell what is easy to sell. Pay attention to this. If it is easy to sell, you're on to something. What is closing these sales? You likely have a compelling Because.

Bob didn't set out to repair Audis and Volkswagens. He grew that specificity from listening to and learning from his customers. He was observant. There were a lot of those customers available, and narrowing his focus grew his business.

What trends do you see in your business? Which customers become long-term clients? Who is the most profitable?

Who do you really enjoy working with? Where will you put the messaging after you create it? How will you go to market? Which customers are your ideal prospects? How will you find your ideal customers and the right people within those companies?

## Specificity Clarifies Your Message

When I was the brand manager of Coors Light, we had millions of potential customers. Consumers of all kinds drink light beer. Even so, narrowing our focus was a powerful tool.

Think about this creative challenge. Your assignment is to make a commercial about light beer. What will your commercial be about? What would the commercial say to convince me to drink your beer vs. any other beer? If you're thinking about a universe including everyone, this question is unwieldy. You could say just about anything. Where do you start?

What if I told you that 75 percent of all the beer in the United States is consumed by men? Wow. That's a valuable *insight*. It narrows the focus of your *ideal customer* to men. While that insight is helpful, it still leaves an exceptionally large sandbox for your ideas. During much of the '80s, '90s, and 2000s, beer companies made raucous ads that appealed to male egos, were funny, or both. While the ads were targeted at men, they generally had nothing to do with the beer.

What if you narrow your focus further? What if you narrow it by age? It turns out that twenty-one- to twenty-four-year-old men drink about eight times more light beer than all other men.[1] This is helpful, but you still end up with the same kind of advertising, maybe just more obnoxious. So, let us narrow the focus further. Research shows that one of the top things these men want from light beer is for it to be cold. It may seem obvious, but it's actually a top insight. Now, your assignment is to make an ad that appeals to twenty-one- to twenty-four-year-old men but is specifically about their beer being cold. Now we're on to something. Do you see that as you narrow your focus, your creativity increases? The smaller you make your sandbox, the bigger your ideas will be.

## The smaller you make your sandbox, the bigger your ideas will be.

### Specificity Attracts Customers

Picture yourself at a party. You're walking around meeting people. You meet someone and ask what they do. They say, "I'm a financial planner." What do you want to do? Yes, everyone has the same reaction—run. You know what's coming next: "Hey, we should grab coffee." Not only do you not want to grab coffee, but you are also not inclined to make any referrals.

What if the financial planner increases their specificity? "I'm a financial planner, but I only work with a very specific kind of client." Now, instead of wanting to run, you want to know what kind of client they work with. They have you leaning in instead of leaning back simply by using specificity. You're seeking more information just because they have narrowed their focus.

Now they tell you that they only work with self-made millionaires. Their clients have a specific life situation that they specialize in helping them navigate. They only work with a small number and are solely focused on this unique type of client. Now you might be thinking that you *are* a self-made millionaire, or you know someone who is. "My aunt just sold her company; she should really talk to you."

Instead of making people want to run, they are drawing them in and getting referrals by being specific about their ideal customers. They have made it easier for people to know who they should refer to them—and to know what to say on their behalf. People naturally want to be helpful. It's our job to make it easy for them to *be* helpful. Specificity attracts customers and increases referrals because people believe you can deliver results.

## Specificity attracts customers and increases referrals because people believe you can deliver results.

Of course, every financial planner would love to only work with millionaires, just like every realtor would love to sell million-dollar homes. But that is not the only specialization that works for financial planning. There are other financial planners I've worked with who focus on police officers or university professors, and one in Michigan who focuses on workers on the Ford assembly line.

You can see the benefits of specificity not only in referrals but in the efficiency of your business. If you only focus on university professors, you deeply understand their situation. Things like the tenure track, their salary, and their mindset. Many professors may even have similar life objectives.

Specificity works particularly well in professional services or any industry with a lot of regulation that limits your marketing and sales messages, such as financial planning, insurance banking, credit unions, or law.

Specificity closes sales because it increases certainty, elevates trust, and speeds customer decision-making. Specificity is a powerful Because that gives customers confidence in their decision and increases their belief that you will deliver.

## Specificity closes sales because it increases certainty, elevates trust, and speeds customer decision-making.

Specificity also makes it clear how to refer you. Narrowing your focus will grow your business by giving customers clarity about what to say and to whom. It will also ensure that everyone inside your organization knows who you serve and why you are the best choice.

Narrowing your focus can be one of the most challenging and most valuable things you can do as a business owner. It increases your focus, hones your messages, and can produce valuable innovations. Clarity about your ideal customers is step 1 in the Because Framework. This specificity then drives steps 2 through 4: uncovering insights, promising outcomes, and creating Becauses.

STEP 2

# What Are
# Your Insights?

A COUPLE OF years after the Blockbuster Video bankruptcy, I interviewed the person who had been their SVP of research and marketing planning and eventually the head of marketing during their final years.[1] The job of the research department is to give the executives *insights* about their customers that will help them sell more and be more profitable. He shared with me what unfolded during that time.

When the research department presented the information about how much consumers liked receiving DVDs through the mail from Netflix, the executives at Blockbuster had a telling response, which we can paraphrase as "What do you recommend we do with our 9,000 stores and the 85,000 people who work in those stores?"[2] The executives chose to ignore some critical customer insights.

Blockbuster tried many strategies to compete, but none of them worked because they didn't focus on the underlying insights. Blockbuster even tried dropping late fees[3]—but that didn't help. It reduced revenue and depleted store inventories since people didn't bring their movies back. So late fees returned.[4]

Blockbuster was unable or unwilling to obsolete its model during competitive disruption. At one point, Netflix even tried to sell itself to Blockbuster, but Blockbuster passed on the opportunity that could have saved it.[5] Blockbuster was trying to make an old model work in an industry that had been disrupted. By 2012, Netflix had bankrupted the once $6 billion Blockbuster.

No matter how large or powerful your company is, you cannot succeed if you ignore your customers. The best companies invest in listening to their customers, understanding their shifting wants, and acting on those insights.

This historic case study teaches us an important foundation of business: *Give your customers more of what they want and less of what they don't.*

## Give your customers more of what they want and less of what they don't.

Yes, this seems exceedingly obvious. Almost comical. But this is the foundation of the Because Framework—understanding customer insights.

Think about this: What did you not like about Blockbuster? My audiences regularly name three things:

1. I had to go to the store.
2. The movie I wanted was out of stock.
3. They charged me a late fee if I didn't get it back on time.

At the time, these things just seemed normal. Get in your car, drive to the store, find a parking spot, look around for videos, find out all the good ones are out of stock, get one you didn't want in the first place, forget to bring it back, and pay a late fee. And if you are from my generation, "Be Kind, Rewind."

Some customers liked the in-store selection experience, and they liked picking out a movie on the same day they wanted to watch it. But for many, the only thing they liked more than walking around the store was *not* walking around the store. A great company truly listens to their customers, then leverages those insights to give their customers more of what they want and less of what they don't.

Netflix asked:

- What if you never had to drive to the store again?

- What if we had an unlimited selection of every movie you want?

- What if you could send it back whenever you want? No late fees.

They took down a multibillion-dollar brand in just a few years by using that simple, foundational idea: give your customers more of what they want and less of what they don't. Physical stores, thousands of employees, a business model that generates profit from something customers don't like— late fees. In hindsight, it was a recipe primed for disruption.

What will you do to disrupt your business model before someone does it for you? Where in your business do you generate revenue or profit from something your customers don't like? To be influential, you must understand the world from the perspective of the people you are influencing. What matters to them? Everything is built upon this understanding.

## Uncovering Your Insights

To uncover your customer insights, ask yourself these six questions:

1. What do they want more of?
2. What do they want less of (their frustrations)?
3. What do they hope for?
4. What do they fear?
5. What problem are they really trying to solve?
6. What are their current perceptions/beliefs?

What do your customers *hope* will happen if they give you their money? What do they *fear* will happen if they give you their money? Even more powerfully, what do they fear will happen if they *don't* choose you and they choose a competitor? What problem are they trying to solve, and what do they already believe about your industry, your business, or the solution they are looking for? Make your list of customer insights, one for each type of customer or individual you need to influence in your sales journey.

Brain science shows us that people are about twice as motivated to *avoid what they don't want* as they are to get what they do want.[6] We know what we want our business or life to be like after we buy, but we fear what it will be like if we make the wrong call.

**People are twice as motivated to avoid what they don't want as they are to get what they do want.**

While these questions seem simple, the answers are the foundations of your ability to influence. When leading company brainstorming sessions, I regularly help teams generate a list of thirty to sixty insights.

When companies brainstorm insights, a common mistake is thinking about insights in terms of what your company delivers to customers. Remember, the insights are about *what they want*, not about *what you do*. Be sure to focus on your customers from their perspective.

## Insights are about what customers want, not about what you do.

Think about this: What are the top objections you hear when selling directly to customers? What are the reasons they give you when they say no? These are insights. What are the things that frustrate you about your customers? These are insights too. Anticipating objections is a key part of any sales process and helps uncover powerful insights.

Sometimes during in-company sessions, the brainstorming about insights gets heated. People say, "Yeah, but our customers think…" or "Our prospects always…" or "They don't understand that…" These are your customers' current perceptions or beliefs. Sometimes customers frustrate us. But those frustrations provide great insights. You may like your customer insights, and you may really *not* like them, but insights are not good or bad. They are just opportunities to enhance your message or innovate your business.

Where do you need to break through a gatekeeper in your sales process? What are your insights about those gatekeepers? You can use the Because Framework to influence gatekeepers the same way you influence decision-makers.

Some insights are rational insights—customers focus on price. Some are emotional—I want to do the best thing for my family. Some are both—I want a car that won't break down, so my family is safe.

When generating your list of insights, remember to consider both rational and emotional insights. Many times, customers want you to think they are only rational. They want you to believe that the only thing that matters to them is low price. They want you to think they are going to pit you against all the other competitors and choose the "lowest acceptable bid." They want to take emotion out of the decision process, so you feel pressure to give them the lowest price.

But in every decision, there are both rational and emotional factors. "I don't want to make a bad call." "I don't want anything to go wrong down the road." "I don't want the hassle of working with someone who will make my job harder, not easier." "I want to look smart to my boss [or my spouse, neighbor, or father-in-law]." By the way, this one seems to be a universal insight that comes up with every company I work with. Their client, customer, or consumer wants to look like a rock star. How can you ensure that your customer will look good for having chosen you?

Customers want to trust that you are going to deliver what you say you will, when you say you will, how you say you will. Their brains are looking for that rational reason to make the emotional decision.

After you have created your list of insights, note which ones are rational and which are emotional. Some of your insights are more valuable than others. Some of your insights are simply customer *expectations*. These things are the price of entry for doing business in your industry. If you are an accountant, customers want accuracy. If you are a restaurant, your customers want delicious food. If you are a bank, your customers want competitive rates. If you are a gas station, your customers want to pay at the pump. Providing these things is just what customers expect. They don't make you the first choice. At best, they get you into consideration. They don't make you special; they make you the same.

> ## Some of your insights are simply customer expectations. Delivering on them doesn't make you special; it makes you the same.

Many business owners talk about things that are the price of entry as if they make them special. "Low prices! Great selection! Friendly service! We care about our customers!" They think if they simply say it, or say it louder, it makes people believe them and want to buy from them. It does not. If you deliver what everyone else does, it does not help customers choose you; it just makes them more confused. Remember, customers don't like to be confused—they want to be certain that they are making a good decision.

### Narrowing Your List: Valuable and Actionable

A list of thirty to sixty insights can be overwhelming. To make the insights useful, there are a few steps that help reveal the top insights.

First, compile a list of every insight on a set of flip chart pages. Combine any duplicate ideas. Importantly, don't combine ideas that are related but not clearly duplicate. Granularity of insights is important later in the process when you're creating Becauses and brainstorming innovations.

For example, some teams are tempted to create one bucket called "customer service." It's true that your clients may value customer service, but there are many insights that fall under this category. Customers may want responsiveness, expertise, a consultative approach, willingness to "make it right," easy communication platforms, access to executives, and many other things. Saying customer service is something they want is not nearly as valuable as capturing those more granular insights. Each of those insights can be a starting point for innovation.

Now, look at your list. Does it seem like a good assessment of your customer? What are you missing? Typically, a de-duplicated list still includes twenty to thirty insights.

## Look for insights that are both valuable to your customers and actionable by you.

Next, prioritize your top insights. Look for insights that are both *valuable* to your customers and *actionable* by you. Which of the insights do you believe are the most important to your customers? Which insights drive their decisions? Which are their biggest frustrations? Now, of those, which can you impact? Which might you be able to impact in the future with an innovation? The insights on which you can deliver become your starting point for influence and innovation.

A simple way to narrow your list is to do a voting exercise with your team. Everyone on the team gets to vote for only five of the insights on the list that are the most *valuable* and *actionable*. Count all the votes and see what comes out on top. Generally, companies end up with between five and ten insights that top the list. That doesn't mean that the other insights aren't important. Each is likely valuable to someone at some point in the sales process, but a few of them are the most important decision factors. You don't need to discard any insights, but focus on your top insights first.

After voting, look for commonalities between your insights. Many times, you'll see that your insights can be combined into a few categories. Feel free to create categories, but retain the individual insights for later brainstorming. These insights can change anything in your company, including your message, sales flow, innovation, hiring strategies, and culture.

## Insights Drive Innovation

It doesn't have to take a long time to uncover insights that will change a business model. Think about the process for buying a car at a typical dealership. What is frustrating about it? What do you want more of or less of when buying a car? What do you hope for, and what do you fear? Regularly, my audiences come up with the same insights in under a minute.

- I don't like haggling on the price.

- I don't like that it takes forever.

- I don't like that they pass me around to all these different people, and I have to go to the manager to negotiate.

Goodness, what *do* we like about buying a car? It seems like not much. Why have dealers taken all the fun out of such a special occasion? Why are they basing their business model on things customers *don't like*?

Schomp BMW in Colorado moved to a simple model and simple promise in 1993: "One Price. One Person. One Hour." This is our price, no negotiation; one person can complete your sale all by themselves; and you can finish in an hour. Genius. Since launching the "One" strategy, their business has exploded. Schomp Automotive Group has expanded to ten dealerships, encompassing the BMW, Mini, Honda, Mercedes-Benz, Subaru, Mazda, Hyundai, Porsche, and Ford brands across three states. When I interviewed Michael Dunlap, a Schomp executive, about their success, I asked him how much of their success came from moving to the one-price, single-contact model. He simply said, "Well, all of it."

They got the insights right and then took action to innovate. They changed their business model to give customers more of what they want and less of what they don't. Of course, they do all the things you expect from a great car dealer— good service, clean facilities, friendly staff, and everything else. But their Becauses are what drive the business. Because there is one price. Because you buy from one person. Because you can buy your car in one hour.

Changing your business model can be scary and challenging. When you make a major strategic change like this, you ideally want to do something that will be hard for your competitors to copy. You want to create something that is valuable for your customers and something that competitors *haven't done, can't do, or won't do.*

Is it hard for other dealers to copy Schomp's model? Yes. To do it, a dealer must change their systems, their incentive structure (no more commissioned salespeople), their training, and their business model. When an auto dealer moves to a one-price model, it impacts dealer margins. Customers love it, but it takes time to optimize the business. However, done well, it's a good long-term strategy.

## What can you do that your competitors haven't done, can't do, or won't do?

There has been a lot of innovation in the auto sales process with companies like Carvana, CarMax, and Tesla leveraging the power of customer insights to build great business models. These companies all do things that are hard for other dealers to copy.

What can you do that your competitors haven't done, can't do, or won't do?

Visit **TheyBuyYourBecause.com** for help finding your Becauses.

### Insights Drive Culture

Angelle Materials is a concrete company in Baton Rouge, Louisiana. There are five other big concrete companies in Baton Rouge. The executive team from Angelle attended one of my executive team workshops. Before the workshop, the team gathered insights from their customers. They talked to their customers to find out what they wanted more of and less of, what they hoped for and feared, and what problems they were trying to solve.

Brian Trauernicht, the CEO of Angelle, indicated that they had come up with two big customer insights.

"First, concrete is very stressful for the general contractor. It's a stressful part of the build because everything is built on the concrete foundation. It must be poured perfectly. The trucks need to show up on time and pour correctly so there are no cracks or weak spots. It's very stressful."

Got it. "What's the second insight?"

"Well, we talked to our customers, and they told us that... well... our drivers can be difficult... contentious... and sometimes kind of scary."

Oh. Wow. That's quite an insight.

Based on that insight, Angelle brought all their drivers in for training. They gave them new shirts, name tags, and cell phones. They gave them business cards with their cell phone numbers on them. They pointed out that they interact with customers more than anyone else in the company. They trained them to get down out of the concrete truck, meet the manager of the project, look them in the eye, and give them their business card. Tell them, "It's my job to make sure that you have a stress-free day." All the drivers completed the National Ready Mixed Concrete Association's Concrete Delivery Professional Certification. They transformed their drivers into brand ambassadors for the company.

This changed the culture of Angelle. It gave the frontline employees pride in their job. It elevated the expectations for their drivers. It gave them clarity about what to do and how to do it. It showed them that the company was investing in them. It made them feel important. It showed them how their job mattered to the company. It changed their customer relationships.

Angelle is growing because they listened to their customers and took action. They leveraged insights to become a better company. Also, in a market where it is hard to find and hire drivers, Angelle now has a reason why drivers would want to work for them—a Because. "Because at Angelle, our frontline drivers are our most important customer contacts. They are why customers do business with us. We only hire the best of the best drivers because those relationships are so important." Angelle changed their entire company culture using a small but very important insight. Insights can help you innovate any part of your company from your culture to your products, services, marketing messages, and sales flow.

What do your customers want more of or less of? What do they hope for, and what do they fear? What commitments are you willing to make to consistently give your customers more of what they want and less of what they don't? What are you willing to do that is different than your competitors and valuable to your customers?

## Where to Find Insights

Uncovering customer insights is easier and less expensive today than it has ever been. When I was at Procter & Gamble, we were always listening, learning, and gathering insights from our customers. P&G was famous for its use of focus groups and large-base surveys. The focus groups would help generate and refine innovation ideas. Then the surveys were meant to predict the real-world success of those new products or innovations. These processes were expensive and took a long time. While I was there, P&G began to shift that model, using new approaches like deep-dive one-on-one interviews and "make a little, sell a little" product testing.

We found that the deep insights uncovered one-on-one were many times more valuable and useful than those from group sessions. Instead of spending tens of thousands of dollars running focus groups with a moderator, an interviewer would spend an hour, two hours, or more interviewing individual consumers.

Then when creating a new product, instead of trying to make it perfect through endless surveys and simulations, we would simply make a little of it and try to sell it, sometimes literally at farmers' markets. Interacting with real consumers with real money was very revealing regarding what would sell and what would not.

Almost any research, done well, can reveal valuable insights that will help you optimize your products and services, create new ones, or altogether disrupt your company and your industry. Today, small companies have as much access to valuable insights as big companies. You don't need to do a focus group or a large-base survey to understand what your customers want more of or less of, what they hope for and what they fear.

## Today, small companies have as much access to valuable insights as big companies.

There are many easy, inexpensive ways to uncover customer insights. Here are eight ways you can start finding insights now.

### 1. Ask Your Customers

As obvious as it seems, the simplest way to gather insights is to ask your customers. You already know them and hopefully talk to them often. Ask them what they want more of and less of, what they hope for and fear. Find out what they wish was different, what frustrates them, and what problems they're working on. Ask about their current perceptions and beliefs. It's a great opportunity to reach out to customers with something you really want to talk about—them.

Customers generally love it. So why don't more companies do it? One reason I've heard is that they are afraid of what they're going to hear. It's true: feedback can be tough, especially negative feedback. But negative feedback is also the most valuable. It is the feedback that inspires change and motivates us to take action. Listening to your current customers is valuable and relatively straightforward. Asking those who are *not* currently your customers can be even more valuable.

## 2. Ask Your Prospects

Ken Gray was the corporate director of innovation at Caterpillar. During his time there, he oversaw the development of their hybrid excavator. Caterpillar was behind in launching an electric hybrid. Many of their competitors had already launched "green" hybrids, basically modeled after what the auto industry had done with hybrid cars.

After years of product development and millions spent on engineering, Caterpillar had an electric hybrid prototype. The prototype was so sleek and beautiful it was nicknamed "Black Beauty."

Before putting the hybrid into production, Ken set out to get some customer feedback. On an international trip, Ken gathered six prospective customers. These were not just any prospects. They were CEOs and owners of large contractors who were not currently buying any Caterpillar products—they were only buying Hitachi and Komatsu.

Ken wanted to learn what competitors' customers thought about Caterpillar's remarkable new green hybrid. It was designed to be an efficient, environmentally friendly machine.

With all the customers in the room, Ken introduced the excavator. When he started talking about green, the customers
spoke up and asked about performance. Ken talked about
the performance and then continued with his pitch about
green. This time, they stopped him and asked about reliability. He outlined the reliability and then continued. Next, they
stopped him and asked about operating costs. The customer
insights about hybrid excavators were emerging quickly.

Finally, they leveled with him: your green excavator is the
same as the ones we already own, and we don't even use those.
The only reason we bought them is because the government
told us we had to. They are not profitable to run because the
performance, reliability, and operating costs are not nearly as
good as our standard diesel excavators. We simply don't want
them. We do value green, but not if it's not profitable. We'd
love to be greener with an excavator that has great performance, reliability, and operating costs.

Ken talked to contractors around the globe and kept coming up with the same three insights. His team had spent years
and millions engineering an electric hybrid excavator that no
one wanted.

Meanwhile there was a skunkworks team at Caterpillar that
had been working on a *hydraulic* hybrid excavator. The project
was underfunded and getting no attention. And it was ugly. So
ugly that it had been nicknamed "Medusa." But Medusa had
superior performance, reliability, and operating costs.

Ken knew what he had to do. He went to the Black Beauty
team and told them their project was not moving forward.
He went to the hydraulic team and told them to get Medusa
ready for production. Caterpillar had listened, learned, and
leveraged their customer insights to create a product that was
in demand from customers. After launch, about one in every
three excavators sold in that size class was a hydraulic hybrid.

Visit **TheyBuyYourBecause.com** to watch a video about Caterpillar's development of the hybrid excavator.

When I interviewed Ken, he said that they had engineered and perfected a product that no one wanted because they had their original insights wrong. They thought green was a big idea. It was, but just less important than the top three—performance, reliability, and operating costs. A perfectly engineered product that no one wants doesn't generate sales. Ken said the linchpin of his research was talking to customers who did not like Caterpillar. Customers who already like your company may be more likely to tell you what you want to hear. Customers who don't will tell it like it is.

---

## Customers who like you may tell you what you want to hear. Customers who don't will tell it like it is.

---

### 3. Follow Up after Losing a Sale or a Customer

As tough as it might be, following up after a lost sale is one of the most valuable insight-gathering techniques. Knowing why you won a customer is great, but knowing why you lost the customer is even better. Those insights are a direct pipeline to how to change or improve your product, service, or sales process to land more sales. What did your competitor say or do that won them over? If they went with a competitor, follow up down the road and see how it's going with them.

### 4. Ask Your Front Lines

There is a good chance that the people closest to your customers have the answers you are looking for. Your frontline employees spend more time talking to your customers than anyone. It doesn't matter what their positions are, the people spending time with your customers have insights.

## It doesn't matter what their positions are, the people spending time with your customers have insights.

Many times, when I'm creating an executive session for a company, I'll encourage the senior team to include a person who operates on the front lines. With a prominent law firm, it was their intake person. She was the person between the receptionist and the attorneys. When a prospective client called, she would have the initial conversation to evaluate fit, understand their needs, assess the firm's ability to help, and determine which attorney was right for the next conversation. She had the deepest insights about their prospective clients because she asked them questions for a living. While she was not an executive, involving her in the Because Workshop ensured that the customer's voice was heard during the brainstorming.

### 5. Create a Customer Advisory Panel

A great way to understand your customers is to create an advisory panel. Invite customers or even prospects to be part of a group that gives you ongoing input. Make it clear that their job is to be open and honest and give you tough feedback to make you better. The panel could be made up of a few people who have a deep, ongoing relationship with you, or it could be an email database of ten thousand who give you feedback when you reach out to them. You may meet with them live, virtually, or just through email. Being on an advisory panel makes customers feel special and heard.

## A great way to understand your customers is to create an advisory panel.

I helped the American Institute of Steel Construction create an advisory panel they call the AISC Think Tank. It's made up of industry influencers like architects, designers, and structural engineers. These are people who make decisions about what materials are used to construct buildings. We meet both virtually and live. In setting up the group, we made it clear that the group was not a sales pitch for steel. It was created to listen, learn, and understand the world from their perspective.

### 6. Use Surveys and Social Media

These days, survey technology is simple and nearly free. If you have an email database (which you should), you can quickly and easily send out short surveys to get insights from your customers.

When I was the VP of marketing at Red Robin, one of the things I oversaw was consumer research. We had over two million people in our email database but a limited research budget. We used the database to ask customers their opinions on anything and everything. What was amazing was that the surveys had the highest open rate of any emails that we sent. On a Tuesday morning, we would send out an email to a few thousand people with the subject line "We want your opinion," and before noon, we would have all the responses we needed. Do you know what your customers would rather do on a Tuesday morning than their work? Anything—including give you their opinion.

### 7. Follow Up after the Sale

After you close the sale, it's a good practice to follow up and see how it's going. But do it with an agenda. What would you like to learn from them? Beyond understanding their satisfaction level, this is a chance to learn anything else you want to know. One of the most important things you can learn is the process and factors they used to make their purchase decision. What was their journey from exploring options to their final decision? What can you learn from their journey to help you be more influential during your sales process?

This follow-up opportunity is a great chance to ask if they are willing to give you a written or video testimonial. You can also ask if they have any referrals, if they'd like to be on your customer advisory panel, or anything else you'd like to know.

### 8. Study Your Competition

As part of gathering insights, it is also useful to study your competition. Which customer insights do your competitors focus on? What outcomes and Becauses can you find on their website or in their marketing materials? What do your customers say about your competitors? Are you focused on the same things, or do you have a unique market position?

## I Wish I Knew™ List

As you uncover insights, you'll come up with things you wish you knew. Creating an I Wish I Knew list is a helpful exercise when creating your research plan. It's a simple technique with four parts:

1. I wish I knew… (what you wish you knew)
2. If I knew it, I would… (what you would do with the information)
3. How will I find out?
4. How valuable is it? (on a scale from 1 to 5, where 5 is most valuable)

### Your I Wish I Knew list is the foundation of your learning and research plan.

I originally created the concept of I Wish I Knew when I was overwhelmed by all the insights I wanted to uncover to inform my decisions as a corporate marketing executive. Where should we focus our time and effort? Your I Wish I Knew list can cover a wide range of topics, including what you wish you knew about customers, competitors, and your own company. Your I Wish I Knew list is the foundation of your learning and research plan.

Here are some examples of insights you may wish you knew:

## Customers

- I wish I knew the rank order of the top insights for our prospects.

- I wish I knew the decision process used by our customers and prospects.

- I wish I knew the top ten objections that customers give us in our sales process when they say no.

- I wish I knew what would be a game changer for our customers if we offered it.

- I wish I knew where our prospects are searching for industry information.

- I wish I knew which competitors our prospects are also considering or already buying from.

- I wish I knew which of our competitors our customers think are the best and why.

- I wish I knew where customers feel like they are wasting their time.

- I wish I knew what keeps our customers up at night.

- I wish I knew our customers' biggest limiters to their success right now.

- I wish I knew what frustrates customers who buy from us.

- I wish I knew the customer satisfaction rates for each of our products.

- I wish I knew which of the four innovations we're developing are the most valuable to our customers, will have the highest sales, or have the highest profit potential.

- I wish I knew why the customers we've lost chose to leave.

## Competition

- I wish I knew the average close rate for leads in our industry.

- I wish I knew how much my competitors spend on marketing.

- I wish I knew what frustrates the customers who buy from our competitors.

- I wish I knew our warranty rate vs. our competitors'.

- I wish I knew the perceived value of what we deliver vs. our competitors.

- I wish I knew our customer retention rate vs. our competitors'.

- I wish I knew how our competitors are recruiting for frontline employees.

## Company

- I wish I knew our on-time and on-budget delivery rates.

- I wish I knew the lifetime value of each of our customers.

- I wish I knew our order accuracy rate.

- I wish I knew how much we invest to close each new customer.

- I wish I knew how much of our new business comes from referrals vs. advertising vs. cold prospecting.

- I wish I knew what percent of our leads we close.

- I wish I knew what percent of our leads visit our website before their final decision.

- I wish I knew which of our customers generate the highest margins for us.

- I wish I knew which of our customers tax our employees and resources the most.

- I wish I knew what percentage of their business each customer is giving us and who they are using for the rest.

- I wish I knew which of our customers are buying only one of our products or services and who could be using others.

This is a sampling to get you thinking about the myriad of things you may want to know about your customers, your competitors, or your business.

The questions listed under "Customers" can be the beginning of your customer insight journey. Start with what they want more and less of, what they hope for and fear, what problems they are solving, and their beliefs. Then add questions from this list and your own brainstorming to create your learning plan. Determine which insights will be most valuable for you and then start listening.

What would you do if you learned the answers to your I Wish I Knew questions? How will you find your answers? How valuable would it be?

Insights drive the Because Framework. Insights are the secret to maximizing influence. Insights will clarify your message, ignite innovation, align your organization, increase your close rate, and prioritize your initiatives. Customer insights will settle debates about where to invest, how to go to market, and who to target.

## Create a Listening Organization

Gathering insights is not just a one-time endeavor. It's an ongoing opportunity for everyone in your company. Insights can come from anywhere. They come from the customers, your front lines, cross-functional conversations, vendors, and competitors. Create a listening organization where everyone is contributing insights and then the best, most important insights are put into action.

> **Gathering insights is not just a one-time endeavor. It's an ongoing opportunity for everyone in your company.**

In 2009, Domino's Pizza launched a new campaign called the pizza turnaround. They produced a four-minute YouTube video that profiled a complete overhaul of their pizza. It included footage of customers in focus groups being frustrated with the quality of the pizza, employees getting emotional, and dramatic background music.

There is a very memorable part where a customer says, "The crust tastes like cardboard, and the sauce tastes like ketchup." Then it cuts to an employee saying, "It's hard to watch." And another saying, "It hits you right in the heart."

The video goes on to play upbeat music and shows the energy of all the employees getting excited to change everything on the pizza. "This is what lit the fire under us." By the end, they have explored dozens of crusts and sauces and cheeses. The outcome is a pizza that they love. Visit **TheyBuyYourBecause .com** to watch.

Over the next decade, Domino's stock price was up nearly 5,000 percent. Yes, you read that right. The stock price went from about $8 at the beginning of 2010 to nearly $400 by the end of 2020. If you had invested $12,000 in 2009, you would have had about $1,000,000 at the end of 2020.

It seems like the ad campaign was about Domino's launching a new recipe. In my opinion, it was actually about *listening*. "We listened to you. We heard you. We care." Over and over, Domino's said that they *heard* you.

Customers today love companies who are authentic, who know their flaws, who listen, and who act. Domino's listened, acted, and then told everyone they did it. Over the next few years, Domino's advertising was all about listening. On their pizza boxes, they had surveys to encourage customer feedback. Today, customers want to feel heard, important, and like their opinions matter. They believe they deserve a direct line to your company.

The great thing is when you listen, you learn things. Challenge your company to become a listening organization. Listen, learn, and then execute based on what you have heard.

Insights from your ideal customers are the foundation. Those powerful insights lead directly to steps 3 and 4, promising an *outcome* that is valuable to customers and then finishing the sentence of influence with your *Because*.

# What Is
# Your Outcome?

M ANY TIMES in business, we talk about ourselves—
about our business. "Let me tell you about what we
do! Let me tell you what makes us special!"

What do your customers care about more than *what you do*? What you do for *them*. Before we talk about what makes us special, we must tell our prospects what we do for them. Then and only then do we open the door to talk about ourselves.

## What do your customers
## care about more than what you do?
## What you do for them.

Since the 1940s, sales trainers and advertisements have been claiming what Harvard Business School professor Theodore Levitt famously taught: "People don't want to buy a quarter-inch drill bit. They want a quarter-inch hole!"[1] People don't want to buy the tool; they want to buy the *outcome* of the tool.

I told this story to a friend of mine, and she said, "I don't get it. I don't want to buy a drill bit or a hole. I want to buy a shelf on my wall with all of my books on it." She makes a great point. What your customers buy from you is the outcome. What they want to buy is what their lives or businesses will be like after their decision.

What is the outcome that you promise to your customers?

## Your Outcomes Come from Your Insights

Your outcomes come directly from your insights. After creating your insight list, narrow it to the top five or ten that really drive customers' decisions. Elevate the ones that are *valuable to them* and *actionable by you.*

### Your outcomes come directly from your insights.

Then translate your top insights into the outcomes you will promise based on those insights. What outcome will you promise that delivers more of what customers want and less of what they don't? What will you do to fulfill their hopes or reduce their fears? What will solve their problems? Turn your insights into outcomes. Make a commitment about what you will deliver.

My first paid keynote was for the National Wildlife Control Operators Association. Yes, there is an association for everything. You might be wondering what the members of the National Wildlife Control Operators Association do. These are the people who own companies that get animals out from under your porch, out of your attic, or out of anywhere you don't want them.

Picture in your mind the typical owner of one of these companies. When I do this exercise with my audiences, they repeatedly say things like "He drives a beat-up old four-wheel-drive truck. He's wearing camouflage. He's wearing big work boots. He's missing a tooth. Oh, and he's definitely a man." Then they give him a name. Usually, it's Billy or Bob or Billy Bob. This description isn't necessarily true, but perceptions are what matter. The first step to customer influence is understanding their mindset—their insights.

What are the insights about customers looking for a wildlife control operator? Who do you suppose is typically making the phone call to get an animal removed from their house? When I was researching the industry, I learned that 87 percent of the phone calls coming into these companies are from women. That is a valuable piece of information.

What insights might you surmise about the woman making the call? You might suppose:

- She wants it done quickly.

- This is a disruption from what she was planning to do today.

- She may have never had this happen before.

- She wants to be sure the animal does not get back in the house.

- She wonders how the animal will be removed.

- She wonders where the animal will go after it is taken from the house. "It's going to go into the woods by a beautiful stream, right?" Sure.

- She fears that someone might come in and kill the animal right in the house. Will it leave a bloody mess?

- She wonders what the children are going to see.

- She does not want someone to wear dirty boots in the house.

- She wonders who the person coming into her home is. Have they been background-checked?

You can imagine she fears Billy Bob showing up in a beat-up old truck, walking into the house with a shotgun, and taking aim at the bat in the attic. Now, of course, that's not what happens, but if she's never called a company like this before, there is a lot of uncertainty. Customers don't like uncertainty. They want to be sure they're making a good call.

With just this short list of insights, you could design a company that would disrupt the industry. You could purposefully create the entire customer experience to show empathy, build trust, and deliver certainty. You could plan every interaction from the first call through your follow-up, including: your pre-arrival communication, uniforms, vehicles, how you enter the home, and how you upsell effectively. Then you'd be able to hire the best frontline employees and train them to deliver the best experience. You could clarify the outcomes you promise and prove that you deliver them differently from any other company.

The outcome you promise could be a safe, clean, humane extraction of animals by clean, competent, trustworthy professionals. Additionally, you can offer re-entry prevention so the animals can't get back in. In fact, one of the most profitable parts of the industry is animal-proofing the entry points. It's an easy upsell based on one of the key insights for the homeowner. "Please get the animal out and make sure they don't come back."

If you were running a business in the industry, creating *outcomes* based on these insights would be easy:

| Insight | Outcome (Promise) |
|---|---|
| I want it done fast. | We have speedy service. |
| Make sure the animal doesn't get back in. | Animals can't and won't return. |
| How will the animal be removed? | We provide safe, clean removal. |
| Will it be messy? | We'll leave your house better than we found it. |
| Can I trust the person coming into my home? | You can trust our professionals. |
| What will my children see? | We're happy to educate your children about the animals and area wildlife. |

Our insights led us directly to these outcomes. You'll notice that the outcomes sound a bit fluffy—like the sea of sameness. It's because we have not yet connected the outcomes to Becauses. This is the number one mistake companies make in their marketing and sales: they make a promise with no proof. They do not finish the sentence of influence, and their messages fall flat.

**The number one mistake companies make in their marketing and sales: they make a promise with no proof. They do not finish the sentence of influence.**

## Outcomes Are Not Enough

Your outcomes come from your insights. Your outcome is what's in it for them. But if you stop there and don't finish the sentence of influence, your message ends up sounding like marketing fluff. Companies say things like (these are real examples):

- We are your trusted partner.
- We are experts in excellence.
- We won't leave until the job is done.
- We save you time, money, and frustration.
- We strive to overdeliver for every customer.
- We're on time, every time.

These are all fine outcomes. They are likely desirable to your customers, and they may even be true, but if you say these things with no Because, they sound like marketing fluff. The ear, the gut, the subconscious, and the brain are not convinced.

The reason these statements don't work is because you haven't finished the sentence of influence. You have delivered a promise but haven't given the proof. Our brain immediately starts to question the promise. "You have higher quality *because...?*"

Try this on your ears. Let's say I've started a pizza company—Gerry's Pizza. Here is my marketing: "Come on into Gerry's Pizza. Our pizza is better." Do you hear how it leaves your brain hanging? If you promise an outcome with no Because, it sounds like marketing fluff. Your brain wants me to finish the sentence of influence. "Your pizza is better *because?*"

## If you promise an outcome with no Because, it sounds like marketing fluff.

Papa Johns Pizza finishes the sentence of influence. Their slogan is "Better Ingredients, Better Pizza." Better pizza is the *outcome*—the promise; Better Ingredients is the *Because*—the proof.

In 1997 when Papa Johns was still a small pizza company, they were sued by Pizza Hut, which took issue with them saying their pizza was better. Papa Johns ultimately won the lawsuit because they used fresh sliced tomatoes and filtered water, and Pizza Hut did not.[2] Now they have a Because—"because the federal court said our pizza is better!"

While the proof it took to win the lawsuit may have been small, specific, and relatively unimportant to the product, their commitment to better ingredients gave Papa Johns valuable clarity as a company. Everyone in the organization was clear about what made them special: the ingredients. If you go to their website today, they still talk about what makes their ingredients better than the competition. This specificity and clarity have served them for decades and resulted in a multibillion-dollar company. Better ingredients is not just a slogan. It's the foundation of their strategy as a company.

This is a simple example. Most of you do not work in industries where you are selling something as simple as a pizza. You are selling things that are more complicated, more expensive, and more valuable to your customers than pizza. That makes your Becauses even more critical. Your Becauses must be believable, important to your customers, and unique to you. Your Becauses must be powerful *proof* that will make the customer believe the promise you are making.

Link your promise (outcome) to your proof (Because)— your rational reason for them to make the emotional decision to buy from you. In the next chapter, I'll show you how to connect your outcomes to your Becauses.

## Your Outcome Can Be Simple

In 2009, the movie *Paranormal Activity* was released. The producers had a challenge: they had almost no marketing budget. And yet the film ultimately earned over $190 million in revenue and spawned an entire *Paranormal Activity* franchise.

How did they do it? What is the *outcome* you want from going to a scary movie? You want to be scared! Yep, a pretty simple outcome. Pay money and get scared, that's the whole transaction. What did *Paranormal Activity* do differently than other scary movies? The movie trailer showed you a real audience being scared by the movie. Go to **TheyBuyYourBecause .com** and watch the trailer. It opens with a shot of people standing in line waiting to watch the movie, cuts to the audience members filing into the movie theater, and then, before they even show you any clips from the film, they show the audience jumping in fear.

They eventually show snippets of the movie, but the focus of the shots is the audience experiencing the outcome—being scared. "Watch *Paranormal Activity* and you'll be scared too." Showing the scared audience demonstrates that you'll get the outcome you want from a scary movie. It gives your brain the *rational reason to make the emotional decision* to see the movie. It gives you confidence that you will get the outcome you are paying for. It gives you a Because.

The production budget for the film was just $15,000. The movie opened in only twelve theaters but expanded to over 2,700 theaters.[3] Now the *Paranormal Activity* franchise encompasses seven films, digital comics, and a video game. It has grossed nearly $1 billion worldwide.

All this started with connecting their outcome to a powerful Because. In this case, the Because was *social proof*. "Those people are scared, so I believe I'll be scared too." People wanted to see what the audience in the trailer was seeing. They believed that they would get the outcome they wanted for the money that they paid. Social proof is just one way you can create a Because. Part III outlines seventeen ways to create Becauses, with case studies and examples.

How do you turn around the camera and demonstrate to the audience that they will get the outcome they want from watching *your* movie? What's the outcome they want from buying your product or service, and what is your proof?

## What Are Your Competitors Unwilling or Unable to Do?

After a keynote to the plumbing industry, I led a workshop for a room full of plumbing company owners. Plumbing is a crowded, competitive, commoditized industry. We all know that one of the frustrations with in-home service providers is that they come to your home in a "window" of time. "We'll be there between eight a.m. and noon." This is basically saying that the plumber's schedule is more important than yours. The fact that they cannot predict how long jobs will take becomes your problem. The model assumes that you have half a day to hang around waiting for them to show up. But what choice do you have? Do you want your problem fixed or not?

As we worked on outcomes, one of the owners in the room shared his promise: we commit to a time, and we show up on time, every time. I asked, "What's your window length?" He said, "You don't understand. We don't have a window. If we say we'll be there at nine a.m., we come at nine. No window."

"Wow. What happens if you're late?" I asked.

"We give you $50."

There was a lot of verbal rumbling in the room. One of the other owners in the room asked how they manage it.

He said that at first it was a disaster, but over time they got much better at arriving on time. The owner indicated that it was tough, but since they started, they have figured out how to do it well. It is what they have become known for. "We show up when we say we will, or we'll pay you."

I asked him how often his customers push back on his pricing. He looked at me and simply said, "Well, they don't really. Our customers aren't focused on our price; they're focused on the value of their time. We give them certainty about their time so they can get back to work or get on with their day. They trust us. They don't mind paying a fair price when we value what they value."

When the plumbing company owner explained that they didn't have windows and they would pay the customer $50 if they were late, one of the other owners in the room called out, "Well, I'm not going to do that!"

Exactly.

What are you willing to do that your competitors can't do, won't do, or haven't done? Things that are hard or inefficient for you, but valuable to your customers, can lead to disruptive innovation. A simple outcome like "We show up when we say we will" is the result of acting on insights. How can you transform your company to do what is good for customers, not what is good for you?

Challenge your team to uncover ideas that would be valued by your customers but that nobody in your industry is willing to do. Things that are not easy for your company but are important to your customers are a way you can create differentiation that sticks.

## Things that are not easy for your company but are important to your customers create differentiation that sticks.

This type of innovation is particularly valuable because if it's hard for you, it's also hard for your competitors and they may not be willing or able to copy you. That is innovation worth pursuing.

Approach the problem from multiple angles. Eliminating the window is only one solution. How else might a plumber value their customers' time? Maybe they could have a two-hour window and then narrow the window as the time gets closer. Maybe they can commit to call or text them when the plumber is about thirty minutes out. That way, the customer can leave work and meet the plumber without waiting all day. Maybe there could be a tracking app so they can see where the truck is and how many stops before they get to your house, with times updated along the way. Insights ignite creativity and innovation. First, gather your insights and then create an outcome based on what is valuable to your customer.

This plumber focused on the outcome of saving his customers' time and connected it to a powerful Because. Because we'll show up on time, and if we don't we will give you $50. There are many other outcomes that plumbers could choose. What outcomes are most important to your customers based on the insights you've gathered?

List the top five or ten outcomes you promise. Which are your competitors already promising? Do they prove them with compelling Becauses? Are there gaps where you could deliver a unique outcome with a convincing Because? Create a matrix of all the key promises made by competitors. Which can they prove? Which simply sound like marketing fluff? If you were the customer, which would seem believable to you?

If you cross your competitors' credible outcomes off your list, what is left? Where is the open space? If competitors do have credible differentiation, can you come up with something that is even better, more compelling, or different from what they are doing? This is the foundation of innovation.

Your sentence of influence is not complete until you add your Because. Making a commitment and a promise is good, but it must be backed up with proof. Evaluate your sales and marketing language. Are you promising an outcome with no Because? Are you leaving your customer's brain hanging? Are you swimming in the sea of sameness?

If you want to sell more, focus on customer insights, the outcomes you can uniquely provide, and then finish the sentence of influence with your Because.

# What Is
# Your Because?

A T P&G, Coors, and Red Robin, I influenced customers to buy billions of dollars' worth of cleaners, beer, and burgers. All the marketing I did on those brands included one consistent strategy. Whether you're influencing customers to buy using your website, a video, one-on-one meetings, proposals, or referrals, this strategy will work for you.

**It is your Because.**

Your Because finishes your sentence of influence. Your insights become your outcomes. Your Becauses prove you will deliver those outcomes differently or better than your competitors.

Regardless of how you go to market, your Becauses will make what you say more influential. They will give your customers certainty about why they should buy from you. They will make your sales force and your referral sources clear about what they should say about you. They will inform and guide your innovation, generate referrals, and close sales. Your Becauses make what you say more *believable* and more *repeatable.* Your customers believe you are going to deliver what you say and know how to repeat it to others.

## Your Because makes what you say believable and repeatable.

Your customers want confidence that they're making a good decision. They want proof. Proof they could use to convince someone else—their boss, their board of directors, their spouse, or their neighbor. Your Because provides the proof.

### The Foundations of Because

In the late 1970s, Dr. Ellen Langer did some ground-breaking, often-cited research on influence. Langer is the first ever female tenured psychology professor at Harvard.[1] She studied how people were influenced to say yes.

In her research on influence, she used a Xerox machine in the Graduate Center library at the City University of New York, where the coauthors of the study, Arthur Blank and Benzion Chanowitz, were studying. There were often people waiting to use the machine. In the experiment, they had a student try to cut in front of the line by saying different things to see which things were the most influential.

For the first group, the student made this request: "Excuse me, I have five pages. May I use the Xerox machine?" Sixty percent of the time, they let the student cut in line. This is our benchmark. Note there is no *reason*, just a simple, small request. In the second grouping, they gave a reason. They said, "Excuse me, I have five pages. May I use the Xerox machine, because I'm in a rush?"

This time, 94 percent of the people let the student cut in line. In a third iteration, they used a small request and a nonsensical Because: "Excuse me, I have five pages. May I use the Xerox machine, because I have to make copies?"

Really?

Still, 93 percent of the people let them cut in line!

Why does this happen? The study demonstrates that in *simple* situations with a *small* request, our brains are running a script, looking for any reason to say yes. We are triggered to say yes simply because there is a reason. Any reason will do, even if it is nonsensical. This part of the study famously opens Dr. Robert Cialdini's book *Influence: The Psychology of Persuasion*.[2] Cialdini's book is an international bestseller with over five million copies sold.

It almost makes it seem like you can trick customers into saying yes to you just by inserting the word *because*. You are probably reading this thinking that would never work for you in your business, with your product or service. You are right. You cannot just insert the word *because* and magically influence people to buy. There is no simple trick to influencing customers, and there is no magic in the word *because*.

## There is no simple trick to influencing customers.

What Cialdini doesn't tell you is that there is a *second part* to the study. In the first part, they made a small request (five pages). The problem is that in your business, you don't make small requests. You likely make big, important requests where clients are investing lots of money, and there is a big impact on their business or their life.

In the second part of the study, they made a *big request.* That's what you do every day in your business. When they made a big request, they found that they could still be influential, but the quality of the Because made all the difference.

**Your Because matters.**

Instead of five pages, they requested making twenty copies. In this case, the research shows that convincing the person to make a big decision was much harder than convincing a person to make a small decision. People were *only* influenced when they used a logical, compelling Because. When they used the nonsensical because, there was no difference between that and having no Because at all.

When we are presented with a big ask, our brain gets involved and logically evaluates the Because. It's no longer running a simple script. You probably make big asks all the time in your business. You sell to customers who are solving problems, running companies, and investing significant money. They want to be certain they are making a good call. A powerful Because provides that certainty.

That's why promising an outcome with no Because sounds like marketing fluff. Your brain, your gut, and your subconscious don't believe it. You must always finish the sentence of influence—insights, outcome, Because. We would all like a shortcut to influence, but in important decisions, there are no shortcuts.

This marries up with Daniel Kahneman's Nobel Prize–winning work on the psychology of decision-making. We do make emotional decisions, but our brains, our gut, and our subconscious are all looking for *rational, logical proof* that they are a good call. Again, your brain needs a rational reason to make an emotional decision.

When you are making a big request, your proof matters. You must develop compelling reasons they should buy from you vs. your competitors.

As you elevate your awareness of the Because concept, you may start to see Becauses everywhere. You will begin to see when companies are using a Because and when they are not. You will have a keen understanding about how you are being influenced and, importantly, how you can influence others.

## When you are making a big request, your proof matters. Your Because matters.

Do you know your Becauses? Do your employees know your Becauses? Do your customers know why they should buy from you vs. your competitors?

### Your Becauses Are Your Proof

The magic is not in the word; it is in the proof. Your outcome is about *them*, and your Because is about *you*. It's about something that you do. A unique process, procedure, ingredient, approach, or piece of proof about how you deliver your outcome.

You can't simply say the word *because*, insert anything you want behind it, and make it believable. Sometimes when companies start using the Because Framework, they say things like:

- Because we build the best relationships.
- Because we do what we say we will, when we say we will.
- Because we care more about our customers.

While these statements may be true, they don't include any proof. None of these statements finish the sentence of influence. They don't tell your brain specifically what you do that delivers the outcome you promise. These statements are actually just an outcome sitting behind the word *because*. They don't give your ears, your brain, or your subconscious any proof. Your Because must deliver the proof that you can and will deliver these outcomes.

## Your Becauses are your proof.

These examples finish the sentence:

- We have better relationships with our customers because we are the only [company type] in the industry that schedules quarterly status meetings with our clients to get feedback on how we can improve.

- We deliver on time more often than any competitor because we only use 100 percent full-time employees. We don't use subcontractors. That allows us to keep the timelines and commitments we make.

- We deliver a better long-term patient care experience because our average employee has been here more than ten years, and our annual turnover is under 10 percent.

## Growing Coors Light by $250 Million

By the time I came to Coors in the early 2000s, beer was in the sea of sameness. Beer advertising fell into two simple categories. Either it was based on image and emotion—*Party! Party! Party! Drink our beer and you'll look cool*—or it was funny. Bud Light has made an art out of funny beer advertising with dogs, frogs, and horses.

The impact of the sea of sameness in beer was evident. Everyone was doing emotional, fun advertising, but nobody was gaining any share. At that time, Coors Light was focused on image advertising—what you would look like if you drank Coors Light. We were doing things like Coors Light placement in movies, creating ads that showed wild parties, and sponsoring the NFL. The marketing was not working, and sales were flat.

Coors Light was spending as much as $500,000 just to shoot an ad and was spending $100 million per year on TV media, and even more on sponsorships like the NFL and NASCAR. Do you know what your marketing team will say if you spend millions on marketing and sales are flat? "Just imagine what would have happened if we didn't spend that money." Ouch. The job of marketing and sales is to *increase* sales, not to keep them the same.

During that time, many non-beer marketers were being hired by Coors from big, national brands. I started my career in marketing with Procter & Gamble, which owns some of the largest, most successful brands in the world. P&G believes that every product, piece of advertising, and sales message should have *proof* that the product works better than that of the competition. Even recently, P&G has been focused on "irresistible superiority." It's the intersection between emotion and logical proof of superiority. Neither logic nor proof was anywhere in beer advertising.

In 2004, I became brand manager of Coors Light. The team believed that there must be a better way to sell beer. We had to find a way to break through the clutter and grow sales. Could the methods used to sell laundry detergent, shampoo, or paper towels also sell beer? We began to apply the strategies from outside the beer industry to Coors Light. We spent time understanding our *ideal customers*, uncovering *insights* about them, promising the *outcome* they wanted, and delivering a powerful *Because* to close the sale.

Other than the brand, light beer had become a commodity. Guys will tell you they're "a Coors Light guy" or "a Bud Light guy." But when they take a blind taste test, most of them can't pick their beer out of a lineup. So how do you differentiate in a commoditized industry?

You innovate. We set out to create new Becauses for Coors Light, a commoditized product in a crowded, competitive industry. Since we couldn't change the beer, we launched a lineup of packaging innovations and messaging all designed to finish the sentence of influence. In an industry known for over-the-top ads based on image or humor, we inserted rational reasons to buy Coors Light. The innovations we created grew the business by $250 million per year. Here's how we did it.

### Ideal Customers

Our ideal customers were twenty-one- to twenty-four-year-old men. Men drink about three-quarters of the light beer in the United States, and twenty-one- to twenty-four-year-old men drink as much as eight times more light beer than other men. They are a very ideal customer.

## Insights

What do twenty-one- to twenty-four-year-old men want from light beer? We asked them what they wanted and then narrowed their answers to eight primary insights.[3] They wanted:

- Good taste
- Value
- Relaxation
- Low carbs/low calories
- Socialization
- Refreshment
- Cold beer
- Funny ads

Next, we evaluated what our competitors were already known for. Miller Lite had been saying that it had great taste and was less filling since 1973 when it was launched. Still today, Miller Lite says it tastes great and has fewer carbs and calories than other light beer.

Bud Light was known for funny ads with the dogs, frogs, horses, and "Dilly Dilly." It was also the leading beer for socialization and parties. "You will be cool and people will like you if you drink Bud Light. It's a safe choice." Corona had cornered the market on relaxation.

So, what was left? Value, refreshment, and cold beer.

Cold beer? Really? We had a yearlong debate on the Coors Light brand about whether we could convince anyone that our beer was colder. Colder than what? Colder than the other beer in the same refrigerator? Seriously? No one is going to believe that.

### Outcome

We knew who our ideal customers were, and we had uncovered valuable insights. We analyzed our competition and found a gap. It was clear that the unique outcome customers desired was colder beer. But do you see what we're missing?

A Because.

### Because

Why would anyone believe that our beer was *colder*? What is the rational, logical proof that Coors Light was colder than any other beer? It was not sufficient to just show cold beer in the cold mountains or Pete Coors walking next to an ice-cold mountain stream to convince a customer that our beer was colder. We needed proof. We needed Becauses.

We set out on a journey of innovation. The innovation team created nearly one thousand different ideas. While fewer than ten of those ever made it to market, those innovations made all the difference in the success of the brand.

The first innovation that launched was the Coors Light Frost Brew Liner Can. This was a can with a blue liner inside it. We advertised that it "locks in refreshing, frost-brewed taste." Here's the secret: every aluminum can ever made has had a liner inside it. If you put beer next to aluminum, it will corrode, so there is a liner in the can. Most people never knew the liner was there because it had always been clear. We turned our liner blue, told you it existed, and gave it a name.

In a flat light beer industry where nobody could gain any share, Coors Light can sales grew 5 percent in the first year after we introduced the liner—$100 million of incremental growth because we talked about something we were already doing. We gave your brain a reason to believe there was something special about our product, proof that there was something different and valuable. We gave you a Because: "Because the can has a blue liner."

What is your blue liner? What are you already doing that is valuable for customers but is not front and center in your marketing and sales messaging?

After the Frost Brew Liner Can, we launched the Cooler Box. It was an eighteen pack of plastic bottles with a blue liner in the box so you can fill it with ice. It seems basic, but keep in mind these are twenty-one- to twenty-four-year-old men. Ice. In the box. Brilliant!

Then we launched Super Cold Draft. Coors Light does not freeze at 32 degrees; it freezes at 27.4 because it's got alcohol in it. We created a draft system that would pour Coors Light at 29 degrees. Coors Light poured below freezing.

Then we launched the most well-known of all the innovations: the bottle with the mountains that turn blue when the beer is cold enough to drink. Notice what the bottle does: it gives you valuable information when you need it. You know if the beer is cold enough to drink before you open the bottle.

What information would your customers like to get from you that would be valuable to them?

Putting the thermochromic blue ink on the label changed everything. It changed the advertising, it focused the brand, it motivated the distributors, and it excited the retailers. Most importantly, consumers believed their Coors Light would be cold and refreshing.

When we originally went to operations and told them we wanted to turn the can liner blue, they looked at the marketing team like we were nuts. It was going to cause additional cost, changes on the line, and significant packaging obsolescence. And the liner was *inside* the can—no one could even see it in there.

After the Frost Brew Liner Can was a success, everyone wanted to know what was next. We launched the Cooler Box, Super Cold Draft, and then the biggest hit, the color-change bottle. Everyone was excited to launch a color-change can along with the bottle, but it took the engineers two years to figure out how to print thermochromic ink on the can. They said, "It's not easy to do, but we *will* figure it out."

The entire organization had become aligned, excited, and engaged around the idea of Coors Light being colder. Now they saw the magic of a powerful Because. The marketing team, engineers, operations, sales force, distribution network, and retailers all worked in sync. This kind of organizational alignment is possible for you when you create powerful Becauses.

We didn't change the beer, but we did change the brand. We gave everything a Because. Because it has a blue liner. Because you can put ice in the box. Because it's poured below freezing. Because it tells you when it's cold enough to drink.

**What are your Becauses?**

The packaging innovations changed the trajectory of Coors Light. Coors Light was the only mainstream brand that continued to grow sales during the onslaught of craft beer. When your industry is disrupted, powerful Becauses are how you win against current competitors and defend against new ones.

## Your Most Powerful Tool

Your Becauses provide the proof your customers need to understand why you are better, believe you are better, and then repeat it to everyone else who influences the decision. Your Becauses are the most powerful tool you have to take your customers' focus off price. It's just business: all else equal, customers will choose the lowest price. Your Becauses are what make all else *not* equal. If your Becauses prove that you're different in a way that is valuable to them, then you shift their focus to that unique value and away from price.

## Your Becauses are the most powerful tool you have to take your customers' focus off price.

Your Becauses drive referrals. The reason we don't get as many referrals as we want is because we've made it too hard for people to know what to say on our behalf. They don't know how to finish the sentence "You should buy from them because..." Having a clear, compelling, repeatable Because will increase your referrals because now your customers know what to say. Not only do your *customers* know what to say, but everyone in your *own organization* knows exactly what to say. From the front lines to the executive team, it's clear what you commit to customers and how to influence them to buy from you. It's the foundation of your business.

Becauses also increase trust, which shortcuts decision-making. In our age of cybercrimes, political partisanship, robo-calls, and economic uncertainty, trust is becoming more and more valuable. We do not want to be taken advantage of. In industries like home services and automobile repair, there is widespread distrust. Companies that garner trust outperform those that do not. Customers today are so excited when they finally find someone who shoots straight that they will tell anyone and everyone. Trust turns new customers into long-term relationships.

The entire Because Framework is designed to increase trust from both the customers who know you and the customers who do not. Your Becauses are powerful tools to increase trust with customers who have not yet purchased from you.

## We don't get referrals if we make it hard for people to know what to say on our behalf.

Remember the wildlife control case study from the last chapter? It's a situation where the customer likely doesn't know the company, and there is a preconception about the service providers. Let's combine the wildlife control outcomes we created in the last section with Becauses to increase trust and close the sale:

| Outcome (Promise) | Because (Proof) |
|---|---|
| We have speedy service. | That's because we always hold back two trucks from our prescheduled service runs so they're available for homeowners who have unexpected wildlife emergencies. |
| Animals can't and won't return. | Every one of our service providers is certified and licensed in both animal control and contracting so they can safely remove the animals and expertly fix the entry points. |

| Outcome (Promise) | Because (Proof) |
|---|---|
| We provide safe, clean removal. | We are the only specialist in the region who uses a proprietary eighteen-step removal, remediation, and cleanup process. We'll leave your home cleaner, safer, and more secure than when we arrived. |
| We'll leave your house better than we found it. | We respect your home like it is our own. We always have clean uniforms and wear clean shoe coverings, and our proprietary cleanup process ensures that anything the animals left behind is removed and the area sanitized. |
| You can trust our professionals. | Every one of our professionals has completed our one-year animal removal and contractor apprentice-ship. They are all background-checked, certified, and licensed. They are part of our family so they can confidently take care of yours. |
| We're happy to educate your children about the animals and area wildlife. | Our professionals love animals and enjoy talking with kids about all the animals in the area, including the kind being removed from your home. They come prepared with beautiful educational materials showing the animals in their natural habitat (which is not supposed to be your home). |

Does this sound like the kind of animal control company you'd want coming to your home? What would you say when making a referral to a neighbor?

## Becauses Attract Employees

In addition to attracting customers, many companies also use the Because Framework to attract employees. Today, you need to market to your employees like they're your customers. It's no secret that great employees can be the linchpin to business success. In fact, many CEOs I work with believe that their employees *are* their Because. Hiring the best employees and keeping them can be a challenge, especially when the unemployment rate is low.

> ## Today, you need to market to your employees like they're your customers.

The process you use for influencing employees is the same as it is for influencing customers; they're just a different target. What are the insights of your prospective employees? What do they want more of and less of? What do they hope for, and what do they fear? What are the outcomes you provide to them, and what are your Becauses? Why would a prospective employee want to work for you instead of their other options?

Ask prospects which insights are most important to them. Learn their hopes, fears, and frustrations. Have you created a plan, a culture, and a vision for the future that attracts the best employees?

Just like customers, different employee prospects will want different things. You may find generational differences in what is important to employees. Someone early in their career will likely have different priorities than someone close to retirement. For example, many younger employees greatly value flexibility. Especially if they have young children in school.

Also consider your current employees. How will you retain them? The process is the same, maybe even easier—they're already in your company. What do they want more of, less of, hope for, and fear? To find out, you just need to ask them. Have them help you create the kind of company where they want to stay and recruit others like them.

### Your "Why" Is Not Your Because

Don't mistake your why for a Because. Customers choose you because of *what you do for them*, not *why* you do it. Many companies have spent time figuring out their why.[4] Why you are in business can be inspirational for your employees and maybe even interesting to your customers. But to influence customers to *buy*, to get them to sign the contract and hand over the money, you need to tell them what you do for them and prove that you do it differently or better than everyone else—with your Becauses. Customers don't buy your why. They buy your Because.

## Customers don't buy your "why." They buy your Because.

I work with companies that sell real things to real customers—IT services, accounting, spare parts, hydraulic pumps, construction, engineering, and the list goes on. Customers really don't care why you're an accountant or why you sell hydraulic pumps. They care if you are the best choice for them. They care about what you do differently that makes you a better choice than your competition. Their problem is important, and they want certainty that they are making the best decision. It's your job to help them navigate that purchase journey and get them to choose you.

As my friend Bruce Turkel says in his book *All about Them*, "Here's the ugly little secret about human behavior... people are most concerned about themselves."[5]

## Every Company Can Find Becauses

Regardless of your industry or business type, you can create Becauses for your business. You probably have many good ones already. The Because Framework has been used in businesses including B to B, B to C, professional services, restaurants, and everything in between.

While most companies have Becauses, they are many times buried in the third paragraph on the About page of their website. As I work with companies to uncover their Becauses, they regularly surprise themselves with the quantity, quality, and power of their existing Becauses. Many times they are already there, but they are not being put to work. The Becauses exist but have not been methodically identified, refined, and deployed in the sales and marketing processes.

You will see Becauses everywhere now that you know how to identify them. Even unglamorous businesses can use the power of Because to drive impressive growth. Think about this business: floor mats for your car. When you think of floor mats, what company comes to mind? In every instance, when I ask an audience this question, only one answer is given: WeatherTech. Interestingly, every audience has also been able to name their Because. Because they are *laser measured*.

Every communication you see from WeatherTech includes that one simple, powerful Because: "Because they're laser measured." TV ad, radio ad, or online ad: they all have the same Because. What is the outcome? Superior protection from the elements—snow, rain, and mud. That's *because* they are laser measured to fit your car. They also add in an important second Because in every ad: "Proudly made in America."

WeatherTech has built an enormous, well-known company based on a simple outcome and clear Because. Now they are launching innovations across other parts of your car and your home, building upon their initial success that came from creating a powerful Because.

WeatherTech is selling floor mats mostly through thirty-second commercials on TV. That's probably not how you go to market. Every company has a unique sales flow. In your sales flow, you may have to influence multiple stakeholders over a longer period of time. If so, you have the luxury of using multiple Becauses during your influence journey and matching your Becauses to the audience you're influencing in the moment.

## Creating Your Becauses

Creating Becauses is where the rubber meets the road. You need to create believable, repeatable statements that prove your customers will receive the outcome you are promising. What makes your quality better? How do you add more value? How do you do what you do so well?

These answers probably already reside within your company. They come from your people, processes, procedures, materials, testing, track record, hiring, training, customer testimonials, specialization, or any kind of proof. There are probably many things you already do that are powerful Becauses. If you do things that are unique and valuable, you just need to dig them up and put them in the right places.

Collect and create a master list of Becauses using the seventeen techniques in Part III. When you have them all in one place, look at each and ask the team, "Do our competitors also do this?" That's the critical question I ask during my in-company sessions. As you ask the question, you'll likely get some yeses, some nos, and some "Yes, but... we do it differently or better because..." This will help you uncover the granularity of your Becauses, getting to the core differentiators that are valuable to your customers. If you don't have many, then it's time for innovation.

While *because* is not a magic word, there is one set of words that can exponentially increase the power of your Because. These words make your brain pay attention more than anything else I have found. They are an advanced-level Because strategy. The words are not possible for every company to say, but if you *can* say them, or some version of them, you increase the power of your influence. If you cannot say them today, the words can motivate your company to create innovations that allow you to say them in the future.

**The words are: "*We are the only...*"**

"We are the only data security company that..."

"We are the only restaurant that..."

"We are the only plumbing company that..."

What do *only* you do (that is valuable to your customers)? What do you do that no one else in your industry does, can do, or is willing to do? What do you do in your city, or county, or region that no one else does? Feel free to narrow the scope of your claim so that it is true for you.

"We're the only blacktop company *in the region* who is 100 percent staffed with full-time employees."

Even if you are not the only, and everyone in your industry does a certain thing the same way, it can still be worth saying that you do it, especially if no one else is talking about it. Think about the Coors Light Frost Brew Liner Can. Every beer can had a liner, but nobody was talking about it. We turned ours blue and told you it existed, and sales went up.

"Call XX Plumbing and we'll give you a second opinion about the repair job that another plumber quoted." Even if every plumber is willing to give a free second opinion, the one who talks about it gets the benefit.

## Power words:
## We are the only...

You are the expert in your business and your industry. You know what is commonplace, but your customers may not. It's your opportunity to guide them. It is your opportunity to put your best foot forward by telling them how to navigate their journey.

On the Coors Light brand, we had some existing Becauses and created many more through our packaging innovation. Some of the original Becauses for Coors Light were the fact that *only* Coors Light is Frost Brewed as low as 34 degrees; *only* Coors Light is filtered cold, aged cold, and packaged cold. But we had gotten away from talking about those things in our advertising.

What is true *only* about you and not your competitors? What is true only about you *and* is valuable to customers? Your Becauses can come from any part of your business. They prove that you will deliver the outcome you promise.

The Because Framework is easy to understand but can be challenging to execute well. Many times, when companies are getting started, they struggle to find Becauses that are truly unique. As they dig, they regularly come up with more and more Becauses, until they worry they have too many. Your Becauses are out there; you just need to uncover them and then deploy them where they matter.

While your Becauses are your proof, the entire Framework is important. Great businesses start with understanding their ideal customers, uncovering their insights, promising an outcome, and then proving they will deliver with their Because.

**Your Because finishes the sentence of influence.**

What is the ending to your sentence of influence? The next section covers seventeen techniques for creating Becauses.

# PART III

# CLOSE-UP

Seventeen Techniques for
Creating Becauses

---

# Systematic Proof

I N THIS chapter and the next two, I reveal seventeen strategies for creating your Becauses. You will learn every technique I've ever used to create a Because. If you do it correctly, the Framework can change the course of your business. If you do it incorrectly, you'll create worthless, fluffy language that won't sell anything. I'll show you how to recognize the difference. I am going to show you where your Becauses may be hiding. I will present case studies that demonstrate effective Becauses to help you create yours.

Your rational brain, your gut, and your subconscious can hear whether a message includes a Because or not. Your brain is looking for that *rational reason to make an emotional decision*, and if it is not present, the language sounds like fluff, and it doesn't sell anything.

There are three categories of Because creation techniques: *Systematic Proof*, *Perceived Proof*, and *Created Proof*.

Systematic Proof comes from systems, processes, or proprietary technologies that help deliver your outcomes. Perceived Proof influences customer perceptions so that customers believe your promise is likely to be true. Created Proof comes from new approaches, pricing structures, or marketing ideas that deliver certainty. Explore all the ideas and case studies under each category. The case studies, which come from a wide variety of industries, are included to inspire you about what is possible in your industry and for your company. Your ideas may come from where you least expect them.

Everyone in your company can become an expert on influence. The Framework provides a new language that can align your organization, ignite conversation, focus your debates, and drive innovation. Everyone trained on the Framework will see when Becauses are present and will notice when they're missing.

First up: Systematic Proof. Systematic Proof is something that you systematically do that adds value for your customers. This includes processes, procedures, systems, methodologies, technologies, formulations, ingredients, materials, testing processes, or anything that you've created or systematized to add value and create differentiation from competition.

## 1. Proprietary Processes, Systems, or Methodologies

LINX is an audio-visual company that installs AV for big facilities like office buildings, commercial clients, and universities. LINX has innovated the process of installations in a way that is unique to them and valuable to customers.

In a normal large-scale AV installation, the AV company shows up with massive stacks of cardboard boxes containing every component, cord, TV, rack, remote, receiver, amplifier, and everything else. It is a logistical nightmare. Picture yourself at home unpacking a TV, a receiver, a surround-sound system, a rack, a webcam, all the connection cords, a router, a modem, remotes, and a control interface all at the same time. AV companies do this in commercial environments times twenty, times fifty, or times one hundred.

There are boxes, equipment, and cords everywhere. There is a lot of trash that could get mixed up with the small bags of critical parts. Installers need to assemble all the disparate technologies and parts into a system that operates perfectly. Parts regularly get lost or even stolen during the install, causing additional costs, delays, and frustration for everyone involved. Additionally, the AV installation happens at the end of the construction process. Often, timelines get crunched based on earlier delays that have nothing to do with AV.

This is what AV companies deal with on every major project. LINX has created an innovative process for installing AV equipment at scale. They never take all the boxed equipment to the construction site. Instead, they construct every system in their own staging area, where they control the space. By assembling the systems in advance, they ensure they connect, function, and operate flawlessly. They perfect each system and then package it into a modular container so that it is ready to install quickly and easily on site.

If you think about it from the standpoint of the general contractor (who hires the AV installer), LINX has cut out a massive amount of time, waste, garbage disposal, and uncertainty from the contractor's flow. There is no rework when things don't function or connect. There are no missing parts and no forgotten pieces. And importantly, there is certainty under crunched timelines.

You can see how LINX has leveraged customer insights to focus on the outcomes of speed, efficiency, and certainty. Their Because is centered on their unique process of staging, assembly, and prepackaging, which their competitors do not do.

LINX has also innovated how they deliver services *after* the install. Today, across many industries, much of the profit is not earned from the initial sale but from the ongoing service after the sale. LINX created a new way to provide ongoing AV services.

Have you ever been in a conference room where you plug in your laptop, and it just doesn't work? What happens next? You run around to figure out who the AV person is so they can get your presentation up and running. Either AV is somebody's second job, or if it's their primary job, they're busy fixing somebody's computer when you need them. Half of your hour in the conference room is gone before anyone can make the system work.

LINX has solved this problem. Not only do they create and install the systems, they continue to support them—virtually. The system in the conference room or classroom has a clearly displayed phone number for assistance. When you call, you are immediately connected to a LINX professional who understands how that system works and can assist you on the spot. They help you make it work exactly the way that it is supposed to. They can tell you how to plug your computer in, turn it on, and make the sound work. They can connect virtually to the system so they see what you see. There is always someone on call.

LINX ensures that your technology works when you need it (outcome). That's *because* there are experts on call when you need them. That's *because* they built the system, so they know how to make it work. No waiting, no calling the AV person, no wishing that they weren't at lunch or they weren't on vacation that week. LINX is growing because they have taken customer insights, turned them into valuable outcomes, and supported them with powerful Becauses. LINX has created proprietary systems and workflows based on the insights of their customers. What systems can you create or improve?

## 2. Proprietary Technology

Proprietary, often patented technologies are the foundation of Becauses for many companies. Proprietary technology is unique to you and ideally hard for your competitors to copy. As you innovate and create new Becauses, be sure to explore which innovations may be patentable or kept as trade secrets.

One of my clients, Critical Start, has created a powerful, patented technology in the IT security space. They work in an area called managed detection and response (MDR). This is the system that IT professionals use to monitor attacks and ideally prevent breaches of their networks. Historically, these systems have sent alerts to the IT staff monitoring the system. The alerts are prioritized in tiers. The idea is to alert the staff when something bad is happening. The top-tier alerts are the ones that require attention. At least that's the hope.

What really happens is the IT staff eventually becomes overrun with alerts. They do what overwhelmed people do; they start to create their own processes to manage the inflow of alerts. They may create email filters to automatically file low- and medium-priority alerts. But what if a new kind of intruder gets allocated as a medium alert? Now your system is not secure, and that is a big problem. Being overrun with alerts is annoying to IT professionals who want to do the job they were trained to do, not sort through an inbox full of alerts.

**The *insights* from security IT professionals:**

1. **We must not have a breach.** This is critical to companies and is the whole point of having security software and a security staff in the first place.

**2. Our staff is overrun with alerts.**

- They have a high level of annoyance from filtering through false positives. It's a mundane task and not good for employee retention.
- Analysts want to be doing work that matters.
- Analysts stop monitoring alerts. The alerts are simply filed or filtered.
- Analysts fear that they're going to miss something.
- The alerts are happening faster and more often, but the monitoring budget is not growing.

**3. Acquiring, retaining, and training qualified security professionals is a challenge.** Analysts are constantly being recruited away.

Critical Start developed a proprietary technology that addresses all these insights with a whole new way to process alerts in IT security. Their system does not simply *prioritize* alerts; it analyzes and *resolves* every single alert. How can it do that at scale? It literally learns as it encounters threats. It gets smarter and smarter over time.

With the help of the client's IT professionals, the system learns about every threat that it has not previously encountered. Then its decision engine resolves events based on the validated knowledge. The system leverages the new knowledge learned from the IT professionals. It also uses the knowledge generated from over two billion resolutions since it was created. The system is the *only* MDR that gets smarter as it works.

The technology delivers on each of the client insights. It catches breach risks that other systems may not, it reduces staff alerts, and it allows IT staff to focus on their expertise, not managing alerts.

Critical Start's technology catches breach risks that other systems cannot *because* it treats every security event as equal. No prioritization. Unlike their competitors, they "unprioritized" their system. Their Trusted Behavior Registry enables them to put their trust-oriented approach into action by automatically resolving what is known-good and can be safely trusted first—shifting focus to unknown alerts for triage and quick resolution.

Over time, their clients get fewer and fewer alerts as the system learns. The system can eventually resolve 99.96 percent of security events, elevating the truly critical events in real time. It only notifies the analysts when it encounters something it hasn't learned about previously. It reduces the frustrations from the security analysts about being overrun by alerts and feeling overwhelmed. The analysts become security experts again, instead of alert managers, so analyst job satisfaction and retention goes up. What proprietary technology could you create to help deliver on your customer insights?

### 3. Unique Formulations, Ingredients, or Materials

Formulations remind me of my days at Procter & Gamble. When the Ivory soap brand was launched, it was all about purity. By 1895, advertisements were saying "Ivory Soap: it's 99 $^{44}/_{100}$ percent pure. So pure it floats." Is pure soap better? It was probably a much bigger deal in the late 1800s. It created differentiation from the other soaps available at the time.

Dove soap is owned by P&G's big competitor, Unilever. Dove makes a different claim based on its ingredients. They say Dove is one-quarter moisturizing cream. Big brands are experts at using ingredients and formulations as their Becauses. Ivory is pure. That's *because* it is 99 $^{44}/_{100}$ percent pure. Dove will moisturize your skin. That's *because* it's one-quarter moisturizing cream. Dove is using a claim about the ingredients that makes you believe something about the performance of the product.

Agricultural herbicides are another example of innovative formulations. Since the 1970s, glyphosate (first launched commercially as Roundup) has been used on crops to kill weeds.[1] The herbicide was so effective at killing weeds that it became the most used herbicide for agriculture in the US. In fact, glyphosate worked so well and was used so broadly that innovation and development of competing chemicals was limited for decades.

Since the 1970s, glyphosate has undergone a hundred-fold increase in the frequency and volume of usage worldwide. This is partly because, over the decades it has been in use, many weeds have become resistant to the herbicide, meaning that more needs to be used more often to control the weeds.[2] Some weeds do not respond to it at all. It has become an expensive problem for farmers, impacting chemical, labor, and equipment costs. Not to mention that there has been negative press around the use of glyphosate on crops. But an alternative solution hasn't existed... until now.

Kop-Coat, Inc. is a company that has provided herbicides, fungicides, insecticides, and adjuvants globally to the commercial forest market for decades. Leveraging their technology from forestry, Kop-Coat invented a new adjuvant (additive) for glyphosate that dramatically increases the number of weeds that can be killed and reduces the volume needed for effectiveness by as much as seven-eighths. That means a farmer can apply just one-eighth of the amount and get results on as many as two hundred weeds that have become resistant to glyphosate.

These innovations were made possible by taking knowledge and expertise from one market and applying it to another. Kop-Coat spent six years in the patent process, which included undergoing extensive scientific challenges to prove the product worked as they claimed. Kop-Coat is now positioned to dramatically impact the agricultural market from its roots in forestry.

The *outcome* for the farmer is reduced chemical, labor, and equipment costs. That's *because* you can use one-eighth of the product and kill two hundred more weeds than glyphosate alone. That's *because* it is the *only* product that can do this, as proven though extensive validation and its patent. This was possible *because* the formulation was developed using innovation and expertise from the forestry industry newly applied to agriculture.

You can see that Kop-Coat has many Becauses to use in its sales process. When I worked with Kop-Coat, we created well over a dozen Becauses. What ingredient, formulation, or materials claim can you credibly make that supports the performance of your product or service? How valuable is your formulation to customers? What other markets need what you sell to your primary market?

## 4. Quality Substantiation, Testing Process, or Certifications

How do you validate that your product is going to be the quality you promise? What are the details of your testing process? Do you test your quality differently than your competitors? Do you have a more complete, more extensive, or higher-tolerance testing process?

In many industries, traceability has become important. If there ever is a quality issue, they can trace where it originated so they can quickly diagnose the problem and keep people safe.

When distributors and retailers are considering carrying your products, they will want to know about your ability to substantiate your quality. Customers today want more detail about where your products are made, where the raw materials are sourced, and even your impact on the environment. It's one thing to say, "We have high quality." But that falls flat until you substantiate your quality with Becauses.

Auto dealers and repair shops are known for their detailed, one-hundred-point inspections. Many manufacturers tout their ISO 9000 certification. ISO 9000 and other related certifications are published by the International Organization for Standardization, an independent, nongovernmental international organization. It proves that a company meets these standards in its quality program.

In the auto industry, crash tests validate the relative safety of cars. The Insurance Institute for Highway Safety was established in 1959 as an independent, nonprofit scientific organization dedicated to reducing the impact of motor vehicle crashes. It's famous for crashing cars and reporting the results. Vehicles are rated for safety based on performance in several tests, and the best performers carry the Top Safety Pick+ or Top Safety Pick designation.

You can use proof of your internal processes, the expertise of your employees, your track record, third-party credibility, or many other techniques to demonstrate your quality. In what ways can you prove your quality?

PROOF TYPE 2

# Perceived Proof

PERCEIVED PROOF is any kind of proof that influences customers' *perceptions* so they trust your promise. These perceptions make us believe that what you are saying is likely to be true based on the correlating information you are providing. Perceived Proof can include things like exclusivity, specialization, company size, statistics, social proof, visual proof, and third-party credibility.

## 1. Specialization

Specialization helps you focus on your ideal customers and is also an important Because technique. It is one of the most powerful ways to increase customers' trust and shortcut their decision-making. If you specialize in the exact problem I'm trying to solve, I believe you can solve it. I trust that you've seen situations like mine before and know how to handle it expertly and efficiently. Specialization also makes it easy for people to know how to refer you, and it increases the level of trust about what you do. Are you specialized enough that you exclude some types of customers?

- We are a repair shop that specializes in Audis and Volkswagens.

- We are a financial advisory firm that specializes in tax strategy for business owners.

- We are a builder that exclusively builds fast food restaurants.

There is an insurance agent in Miami who exclusively insures homes over $10 million in value. He insures almost every house over that price in the entire region.

Specialization delivers many other valuable benefits to your business. It increases the ease of uncovering and understanding your customer insights. It provides focus, making you more efficient and increasing your margins. It elevates your expertise in the tools and techniques to do what you do. It reveals innovation opportunities. It increases your close rate because prospects believe you're an expert and trust that you can deliver.

Specialization also helps you add value through consultation with your clients. If you specialize in a certain customer type or industry, you become a valuable resource to those who need that knowledge. Recently I completed a major kitchen renovation. I started by using a generalist designer, but when I switched to working with a kitchen-specific designer, she added dramatically more value in far less time. She knew every answer to every question immediately. In a two-hour consultation, she added more value to my process than my original designer had in weeks.

Specialization empowers you and your organization to say no to customers that are not the right fit. Many times, these customers take more time and generate lower margins than those customers who are ideal.

Rendina Healthcare Real Estate is a full-service real estate company that does development, acquisition, design, financing, construction oversight, leasing, and property management of, you guessed it, healthcare real estate. Could they do these activities for other kinds of real estate? Certainly, but does their specificity enhance their success? Without a doubt.

Rendina deeply understands the business model, and importantly the real estate model, of healthcare systems. This expertise allows them to provide valuable consultative guidance to the real estate professionals who work in hospital systems.

They build so many outpatient care facilities that they can do it more efficiently and for a lower cost than the healthcare systems themselves. In fact, they are the only external real estate partner that has ever developed an outpatient facility for the Cleveland Clinic. How's that for a Because? This partnership was only possible because of their specialization.

They work with one major hospital system that stopped triple-bidding their development projects—they send all the work directly to Rendina. This level of trust saves lots of time and effort on the part of the healthcare system and creates efficiency and certainty for Rendina. What kind of value would you need to provide for your key clients to forgo bidding altogether? You might think that it's not possible. Rendina did it. Explore the idea with your best client. What's in it for them?

Specialization is a Because that can deliver focus to your organization, increase customer trust, shorten customer decision-making, and increase referrals.

## 2. Size

Being the largest is a Because that gives customers certainty. If you are the largest, lots of other customers must be buying from you. You must be a safe, smart choice. If you are the largest, there must be good reasons why you became the largest.

After you say "We are the largest…," anything that you say next is more believable. It is a relative to "We are the only…"

"We are the largest manufacturer of high-precision screws in the United States." "We are the largest personal injury law firm in Pittsburgh." "We are the largest landscaping supplier in a four-state region."

Being the largest indicates that you likely have buying power, expertise, longevity, many trusted customers, a great track record, more resources, and better managed processes. "We are the largest in-home services provider in all of Dallas. We have more than three hundred trucks that can service your plumbing, heating, air conditioning, and electrical needs."

Read through the following marketing statements. These were all pulled from a search of appliance retailers in Colorado. Tune your ears. Which of these sound compelling to you and which sound like marketing fluff? Which include a Because?

- We are Colorado's largest independent appliance retailer.

- We are Colorado's most complete appliance retailer.

- We are the twenty-fifth largest appliance retailer in the United States.

- We are the premier appliance retailer in Colorado.

- We have Colorado's best selection of today's most desirable appliances.

- We are one of the best appliance stores in Colorado Springs.

- We are Denver's best appliance store.

- We are a locally owned appliance retailer.

This is real language used on real websites for appliance stores. Which of these strike you as compelling? Which of these sound like the sea of sameness? Some of these are better than others. Could you improve any of these with a Because? "We're the best because..."

Note how quick and easy it can be to complete a simple competitor assessment. Become a student of your competitors and your industry. What are other companies saying and doing to try to stand out in the crowded marketplace? Which messages and innovations sound convincing to you? Which are fluff?

Look at *your* marketing and sales materials vs. those of your competitors. Look at your website, videos, proposals, and other materials. Do you have any language that is falling flat? Are you using Becauses?

## 3. Statistics and Track Record

You can use statistics as compelling proof: "98 percent of our projects in the past five years have been delivered on time and under budget." Analyze your performance or other statistics in your company to see where you can uncover proof about how well you deliver. "We are responsive to our customers [*outcome*]. In fact, 96 percent of our customer phone calls are answered by a live person by the third ring [*Because*]."

What statistics can you use to demonstrate the long-term value you provide to customers? Over the years, I've worked with several home builders. Home building can be a crowded, competitive, commoditized market. For most people, their home is their single largest investment and many times where a lot of their wealth is stored. So, of course, new home purchasers want their home to be a good investment that appreciates over time. The more, the better.

Many builders are convinced that their homes are *better* than the homes built by others. Better how? Better design? Better construction? Better long-term value? If it were a better long-term value, that would be desirable for a customer.

But how would we *prove* such a thing? Statistics.

To be a better long-term value, the house must have either lower maintenance cost or higher appreciation. It would be amazing if a builder could prove that their homes appreciate more over time. Do you suppose that homes built by some builders appreciate faster than those built by other builders? That seems possible.

What if a home builder dug into the data to prove that their homes do appreciate faster than competitors' homes, faster than the surrounding neighborhood, or faster than other homes in the city or state? Picture billboards that say "XXXXX-built homes. The fastest appreciating new homes in the state of Wisconsin." It would certainly make home buyers take a second look. It might drive them to your website or development to learn more.

If you could say your homes have appreciated 10 percent faster than competitors' homes, it would be much easier to sell your homes, even in a crowded market. It would not even be that hard to dig up the data, given that real estate transactions are public.

Many times, there are powerful Becauses in the data residing within a company or industry. It just takes some time and effort to find and analyze that data. What success statistics do you have in your company that can demonstrate your track record of success? Work with your team to dig up every compelling statistic that exists within your company.

This is a great opportunity to create an I Wish I Knew list. What are all the statistics you wish you knew about your company? What is your track record of on-time completion? What is your track record of under-budget projects? How many of your customers have you retained over time? How many of your customers come from referrals? How few of your customers have ever left you to go to a competitor? What is your proof of success, and how does it compare to your industry competitors? What statistics might demonstrate your effectiveness? If you're that good, prove it to me. Analyze your data and find the compelling answers that prove how good you are.

## 4. Social Proof

You can influence new clients by using words from your existing clients or other trusted sources. Use testimonials, prominent clients, trusted experts, or positive reviews to prove you are a good choice. This is *social proof*.

In my role as a professional speaker, my clients want to be confident that I will provide value to their audience and be entertaining on stage. They do not want to make a mistake. They want to look smart for having hired me. They want the audience to be inspired during my session and then to put that inspiration into action after the conference. This is important because it brings attendees back to the event the following year. Those are their *insights*.

We've all been to conferences where the speaker falls flat. That's a big fear for the people choosing speakers. They don't want to hire someone who doesn't wow the audience. It makes them look bad. So how does a meeting planner increase the certainty that they are making a good call? How does the speaker prove to a meeting planner that they are going to deliver?

Go to my website at WhatBigBrandsKnow.com and watch the video on the home page. Does it convince you that I will be a great speaker for your conference, sales meeting, or company event? What parts of the video convince you that I'll deliver for your audience? What Becauses can you find? You will see that my video includes testimonials from clients across many industries saying positive things about me. They talk about how audience members responded to my message and my energy.

Your customers or clients saying you're great is much more powerful than *you* saying you're great. If others have hired you and were happy, then prospects believe they will be happy too. Testimonials are good, and testimonials from impressive or noteworthy clients are even better.

You can combine social proof with statistics to get a double benefit. "Gerry scored 4.9 out of 5 in front of our audience of over nine hundred CEOs and executives." (Yes, this is an actual testimonial and score from a real event.)

You can use social proof in your videos, on your website, in your proposals, or anywhere you can show the experience others have had with you. Online reviews are an example of social proof. In many industries, reviews have become critically important. Customers have become accustomed to researching businesses online before they make the phone call or decision to buy. Great online reviews are a powerful Because and can increase trust and certainty for customers who don't know you.

A UC Berkeley study of Yelp reviews for restaurants demonstrated that a half-star increase in Yelp reviews resulted in a 49 percent increase in the likelihood that a particular restaurant would be completely booked.[1]

Celebrity endorsements are also a kind of social proof. You see endorsements from all sorts of known people, both nationally and locally. While a celebrity endorsement may not be in your budget, it's easy to get testimonials from your clients or customers.

Which of your customers would be best to give you a testimonial? Have them write a couple sentences in an email or online. Even better, shoot some short videos of your clients saying how amazing you are. Ask them to speak about you as if they were telling someone else why they should hire you. These can be great Becauses to use in your sales process.

## 5. Visual Proof

One of my favorite ads is one that you have likely never seen, but you can find it at **TheyBuyYourBecause.com**. It's for a company called Appliance Direct. Appliance Direct is a large appliance store in Florida owned by Sam Pak. If you are in his area, you are probably familiar with his ads. He's quite a character.

Before I tell you about the ad, let's list some insights about people shopping for a dishwasher:

- I want my dishes to be clean.
- I want my dishes to be dry.
- I don't want there to be food left on my dishes.
- I want it to be quiet.
- I want it to be a good value.
- I want it to be economical to operate.
- And, of course, I want to make a smart decision.

Sam has a three-minute video where he shows visual proof of which dishwasher is the best one to purchase. He comes on screen in front of four dishwashers and says: "Here we have three of the best-selling dishwashers in Florida! And a European model for good measure. We're going to test them right here, right now. How well they clean, how loud they are, and how much energy they use." He goes on to say, "The number one complaint about dishwashers is that there is food left in the dishwasher after the cycle is done and the dishes are supposed to be clean." He literally lists all the customer insights right in the ad and then sets out to demonstrate a powerful Because. How does he do it? He puts a cake in it! Yep. He lines up four dishwashers and puts a red velvet cake in each dishwasher to demonstrate which of the four cleans the best.

Without knowing anything about the dishwashers or the ad, are you curious to watch a video that has four dishwashers fight it out trying to eat a red velvet cake? I know you are. This, by the way, teaches something important about making any kind of advertising. You must get the customer to pay attention to the ad. One way to do that is to utilize drama related to the message that you are delivering. You might not even be in the market for a dishwasher, but it sure is interesting to find out which one is going to eat up all the cake, right? It's a good watch.

Regardless of which dishwasher wins, you now believe and trust Sam when he tells you which one is the correct one to buy. He delivers *visual proof* that the dishwasher he recommends does what you want it to do. He gives you certainty you're making a good call. Sam used visual proof to prove it to himself and to you.

It's possible that Sam got a huge truckload discount on these dishwashers. Maybe Sam bought a truckload of them because they actually do work the best. We don't know, but we sure believe Sam and we like him. We might just go in and buy all our appliances there and ask him to recommend which other appliances are the best for us.

Visual proof can work with all sorts of products. R&D Leverage is an industrial mold maker based outside of Kansas

City, Missouri. They make high-end plastic injection blow molds used in manufacturing. The last innovation in plastic injection blow molds was from the 1950s. Blow molds have been made the same way for decades—until now. R&D Leverage has engineered a remarkable innovation in plastic injection blow molds.

The development of this new mold was entirely based on customer insights—frustrations about the way that molds have always performed. One of the challenges with traditional molds is that they allow heat transfer that can damage the parts being produced. With injection blow molding, you want heat where it is supposed to be, and not where it's not.

R&D Leverage has created a proprietary mold that almost eliminates the heat transfer in the mold, using patented thermal isolation technology. When I first learned about this mold, they showed me a thermal imaging visual that demonstrated the heat transfer of a traditional mold vs. the heat transfer of their new mold. You can imagine what this visual looked like. The visual of the old-style mold had red shadowing all through it showing the heat transfer. The new mold had extraordinarily little red shadowing. The thermal imaging was visual proof that this mold was dramatically better than traditional molds.

I don't know how to sell a mold, but I can certainly sell a new-to-the-world technology with powerful visual proof. The thermal imaging shows that the mold is different from the competition's in a way that's valuable to customers. Their mold has seventeen patents, all based on innovations derived from customer insights. Visual proof is just one of the Because techniques they use to sell this remarkable, new-to-the-world technology. What visual proof demonstrates the superiority of your product or service?

## 6. Third-Party Credibility

Grey Goose vodka was launched into the US market in 1997, and by 2004 they were selling nearly two million cases per year. That year, the brand was bought by Bacardi for $2 billion.[2] They were a major player in helping launch the super-premium vodka category.

How did they grow so fast? They used a single piece of third-party credibility and put it in front of their ideal customers. They took out full-page ads in the *Wall Street Journal* and the *New York Times* saying Grey Goose vodka was "rated the #1 tasting vodka in the world."

Number one? Says who? Says the Beverage Testing Institute. What is the Beverage Testing Institute? It's a beverage industry consultancy in Chicago that works with brands to "develop, refine, recognize, and launch the world's best beverages."[3] You read that right. It's a consultancy that launches beverage brands. A possible conflict of interest? I would think so.

The ads gave no information about what the Beverage Testing Institute was, how they did the test, what other vodkas were evaluated, or really any information at all except a big, powerful headline and a small footnote crediting the Beverage Testing Institute. A simple, powerful Because in front of the exact people who want to buy the best of everything. "The best vodka? I'd better try that." They went from launch to a billion-dollar brand in under a decade.

You've certainly seen cars and other things that are rated by J.D. Power. J.D. Power claims to be one of the most trusted brands in America.[4] But what is J.D. Power? It's actually a consumer research company that uses massive surveys and big data to determine consumer satisfaction. It uses that information to create ratings and then sells the rights to use those ratings to brands.

It has become well-known because of the power of third-party credibility. It's famous because companies use its name in advertising. It elevates consumers' trust in the brands and has made J.D. Power a household name. In 1984, Subaru was the first auto company to talk about their J.D. Power ranking in an ad during Super Bowl XVIII. Since then, more than 200,000 television commercials and more than two billion print ad impressions refer to J.D. Power awards annually.[5]

So is J.D. Power credible? It certainly seems so, but what is more important is the *perception* of consumers. There is a reason that thousands of commercials mention J.D. Power by name—because it increases consumers' perception of trust. It demonstrates the value of third-party credibility and of Becauses that use Perceived Proof.

Where does your third-party credibility come from? Does any expert outside of your company rate or rank companies in your industry? Are there any lists or data printed in your industry association or by regulatory bodies?

# Created Proof

C REATED PROOF is proof that comes from product innovations, a new business approach, or marketing programs. Created Proof includes things like unique product differentiators, innovative pricing strategies, customization, added value, unique company structures, guarantees, and new innovations.

## 1. Product and Service Differentiators

Recently I took my Mercedes SUV to the dealership for some service. While I was at the dealership, I noticed some statistics that were very prominently displayed in the service area.

You can imagine that one insight of Mercedes customers is that they perceive the dealership to be expensive. The perception is also that Mercedes replacement parts are more expensive than aftermarket parts. Mercedes understands this insight and has done a great job of describing the reasons you should use authentic Mercedes replacement parts on your car.

In the service department, they had a large display including actual examples of authentic Mercedes parts alongside aftermarket parts. They showed that the parts are not only visually and tactilely different but outlined how they perform differently. The message was clear: if you want your Mercedes to perform like new, you should use authentic Mercedes parts.

Consider these statistical, visual, and tactile Becauses shown on the display:

Wiper Blades: Up to 800,000 more wiping cycles

- **Performance:** Resists extreme ice, snow, and rainy conditions.

- **Safety:** Equipped with a maintenance indicator.

- **Quality:** Precise curvature and pressure points are unique to each model.

- Look at the tip of our wiper blade. Notice the maintenance indicator that alerts you when replacement is necessary.

Cabin Filters: Up to 2x better filtration

- **Performance:** Removes up to 150 percent more potentially harmful particles smaller than 0.1 micron.

- **Safety:** Up to 50 percent better airflow resulting in less window fogging.

- **Quality:** Made with high-quality charcoal layers.

Air Filters: Up to 60 percent more air flow

- **Performance:** High-quality filter material holds up well against snow, water, and other harsh road conditions.

- **Safety:** Protects your engine from harmful dirt particles, gravel, and other debris.

- **Quality:** The soft rubber gasket seals tightly, helping prevent unfiltered air from entering the engine.

- Notice that our rubber gasket is softer and therefore seals tighter and that our filter features more pleats than the aftermarket part.

Use your knowledge of the Because Framework to evaluate each of these statements. Clearly some are better than others. Some are statements that may also be true for the aftermarket parts, but Mercedes is saying them as if they are only true for Mercedes. Some include statistical evidence that there is something unique and superior about the Mercedes part. Others tactilely show that there is something different that you can literally touch and feel about the Mercedes part vs. the aftermarket part.

Also note how, in many places, they indicate the outcomes. What's in it for the customer? The outcome of the cabin filter is that you have less window fogging. The outcome of the air filter is that it protects your engine from harmful dirt particles, gravel, and other debris. They have done a good job at providing you outcomes combined with Becauses. While some are better than others, it's a valuable learning exercise to read them, evaluate them, and see which you find more or less compelling. Mercedes understands the power of Becauses. They've provided a great tool to their service advisors to demonstrate Mercedes' Becauses and close sales. What product or service differentiators have you created?

## 2. Pricing Structure

There are different pricing structures you can use as a Because. One is fixed pricing. When I was the vice president of marketing at Red Robin, I regularly received emails and calls from all sorts of vendors wanting to meet with me. I almost never met with them. Every time I was contacted by a vendor, I would ask them the same question: "Why would I hire you vs. any of your competitors?" I was always looking for their Because. "You should hire us because…"

Many of the companies reaching out to me were marketing or research agencies of one kind or another. I figured if they couldn't answer the simple question about what made them different, they weren't very good marketers.

One research company did break through the sea of sameness. When I asked them what made them different, their answer got me to make a phone call, schedule a meeting, and eventually become a client.

As part of my position, I oversaw all the research at Red Robin. There were lots of things I wanted to research, but we had a tiny research budget. When I asked the research company what made them different, they addressed the exact challenge I was facing. The company, Hanover Research, sent back a note saying they had a program where I could do unlimited research for a fixed annual price. What? I had never heard of such a thing. Given that I had a limited budget, this sounded compelling. And it was different than anything I'd heard from any other company. It was their Because.

I picked up the phone to understand a little more about this. They indicated that I could deploy back-to-back studies— start the next one as soon as the last one was completed. They went on to say that they had research PhDs on staff that would help me design valid studies. They won my business by giving me compelling Becauses.

Fixed pricing is also known these days as a subscription model. I've worked with companies that are providing subscription models across many industries. Today everyone from car washes to HVAC companies is offering subscription models. Fixed pricing provides certainty. It's a powerful

Because that closes sales. Customers get all the value for one fixed price.

Another effective pricing strategy is pricing tiers. Customers like options. Some may be price conscious, while others want the top-of-the-line experience. Again, while I was at Red Robin, we had a pricing problem. We had over a dozen burgers on the menu, but they were all priced about the same— somewhere between $10 and $11.50. The reason the range was so tight is that all the cost of a burger is in the burger patty. The bun, fixings, and condiments were all unique but didn't change the cost or the perceived value of the burger by that much.

Consumers really wanted a lower-cost option, but that didn't work in the business model because every burger patty was the same size and same cost. All the burgers were fresh, never frozen, and each patty was six ounces. There was only one burger in the restaurant that was less expensive—the kids' burger. The kids' burger was much smaller and was shipped frozen, reducing the cost. Hmm...

We created what we called the barbell strategy. On one end of the barbell was the Tavern Double, which was actually just two kids' burgers on a bun. On the other end, we created a few premium burgers with fancy ingredients like garlic aioli and arugula. The Tavern Double was priced at $6.99, while the premium burgers were nearly $15. The menu increased guest frequency at the low end and increased our margins at the top end.

How can you allow your customers to select their level of spend and value? To create the bottom tier, take away some things that are desirable; at the top level, add in things that not everyone will want, but for those that do, they will pay a price that increases your margins. Take a close look at your pricing level, structure, and strategies. How could you innovate your pricing?

## 3. Customization

Customers today want a solution that is tailored to their specific needs. Customization increases their trust that you'll deliver the perfect solution for them. They want you to listen, understand what they need, and deliver a customized product or service.

When I was an intern at P&G, I worked on the Millstone Coffee brand. The concept was personalized coffee tuned to a customer's taste and delivered in the mail. Customers would answer ten questions about their flavor preferences for non-coffee foods, like dark chocolate or milk chocolate, and rare or well-done steak. Based on the responses, we would create a custom mix of beans that matched their palate. It was an early subscription model where subscribers received their custom blend every few weeks through the mail. It's the perfect coffee *because* it's blended to a customer's taste from millions of possible combinations.

Another example of customization is Which Wich Superior Sandwiches. Jeff Sinelli founded Which Wich in 2003 with a commitment to building a superior sandwich. Beyond using quality ingredients and having a great vibe in the restaurants, Jeff created a breakthrough sandwich customization model. You can truly "get your wich your way." When you enter the store, you grab a bag and a red marker. The bag is printed with all of the sandwich ingredients so you can design your sandwich right on the bag by selecting your bread, meat, and everything you want. Then your bag heads down the line, and your custom recipe gets created just for you.

Which Wich has more ingredients behind its line than any other national sandwich chain. So, if you create a Wich that is uniquely yours, it's likely that you can't get the same thing anywhere else. Now, you can also load your custom recipe in their app for ease of ordering. Customization and unique ingredients help Which Wich keep you as a customer and fend off competition in a very crowded, competitive market. How can you incorporate customization into your business model?

## 4. Extra Value

There is an auto parts retailer in central Michigan who dramatically changed his business by adding extra value. Repair shops account for about 70 percent of the volume of an auto parts retailer. They are critical customers. In his area, there were not that many repair shops but two other auto parts retailers. Each retailer provided the repair shops with an interface where they could search current inventory and pricing on every part. Over half of the auto repair shops in his area were owned by one person. When his shops needed a part, they would simply search all three retailers and order from the one with the cheapest price.

The auto parts retailer went to this owner and asked him a question that changed everything: "What would it take for you to buy 100 percent of your parts from me, no questions asked?"

The response? "There is no way I'm going to do that. Your parts aren't always the cheapest."

He said, "Yes, but what would it take?"

He thought about it. "Well, you'd have to have a truck dedicated to just my stores."

"Okay."

"And you'd have to have a driver to drive the truck who is also dedicated to my stores."

"Okay."

"Um. And you'd have to get any part I order to me in under an hour, guaranteed."

"Okay."

And he won 100 percent of the business from the largest owner of repair shops in the area.

What will it take for you to change the game with customers who are constantly beating you up on price? What will you do to provide extra value? How will you get your key customers to stop pitting you against the competition?

There is a roofing company in Denver that upgrades their customer's shingles from mid-tier to top-tier on every job. Normally that is a significant upcharge. Your insurance company will not cover it, but the company upgrades you for free. The materials don't cost that much more, so they do it for every homeowner on every job. It's a powerful Because in a crowded market, and it helps them close the sale. How can you systematically add more value to every client in a way that your competitors haven't done, won't do, or can't do?

## 5. Unique Company Structure

One of my first clients was a large, prominent law firm in Denver. During the years before I worked with them, they had consolidated fifteen different law practices under one roof. One of the partners asked me to deliver my Because presentation to all the partners.

At the end of my presentation, one of them asked me a question: "Gerry, it seems like you're telling us that specialization is really important." I said that it was. He said, "Well, we've spent years assembling fifteen different law firms under one roof. Is that not a good idea?"

I said, "Well, let me ask you a question. How many of your clients use more than one of your practice areas?"

Either the people in the room did not know the answer or they didn't like the answer because no one responded.

Just because you have fifteen practice areas, it doesn't mean your clients find it valuable. It would be valuable to have lots of practice areas under one roof if many of the clients needed to be served in multiple different practice areas. If they don't, the only benefit is sharing back-office resources.

About a year later, one of the partners reached out and indicated that they were splitting up the firm. Her practice areas were peeling off to create their own firm, Ciancio Ciancio Brown. She wanted my help to figure out their Becauses.

During our prep work, she explained that there were still five different practice areas, but they all had one thing in common. They all were focused on *litigation*. If you are going to court, this is the company you want on your side. Their practice areas included business law, family law, divorce law, criminal law, and employment law.

Their unique structure meant that while they had different practice areas, they could collaborate across those areas on specialized litigation strategies. So rather than simply hiring a divorce attorney, you could hire an attorney at a firm that would draw litigation strategies from other areas of the firm. This helps them devise more creative and innovative approaches for their clients. This unique company structure became their "umbrella" Because. Each of their practice areas also created their own Becauses.

Is your company structure the same as your competitors' or unique in some way? How could you create an innovative structure that would be valuable to your customers and be a compelling Because?

## 6. Guarantee

In 1956 Nate Sherman founded the company that would eventually become Midas Muffler. When he first launched the company, he made a guarantee. Some of you may remember this from the advertising in the '70s and '80s. "We guarantee your muffler for as long as you own your car."

They made a guarantee that they would replace your muffler if it failed at any time while you still owned the car. This guarantee is brilliant. The guarantee gives you the confidence that Midas will put on a high-quality muffler and stand behind it. Nate believed that most customers would sell their car before the muffler fell off, so the marketing of the guarantee was more valuable than the cost of the replacements.

Their mufflers may be no different than anyone else's, but with a powerful Because, they grew sales, grew the franchise organization, and eventually sold the company. Today, Midas (the franchisor) does nearly $250 million in revenue and franchises nearly 2,250 locations.[1] It's interesting to note that they still offer the lifetime guarantee, and they've even expanded it.

> In fact, we guarantee all our work. And we're known for our lifetime-guaranteed brake pads, shoes, mufflers, and shocks and struts. Our limited lifetime guarantee is valid for as long as you own your car.[2]

Another company with a prominent guarantee is LifeLock. LifeLock protects your identity and lets you know if anyone unscrupulous has accessed your information. Their guarantee is that if anything happens to your data, they will back you with $1 million in coverage for lawyers and experts.

That is a remarkable guarantee. I don't know if $1 million in legal fees is enough to defend you against having your identity stolen, but it sure sounds like it would be. It gives me the confidence that LifeLock is going to stand behind what they do.

Another unique use of a guarantee is Toro lawn mowers. They have a guarantee front and center on every lawn mower: "Guaranteed to Start."

When I was a kid in the '70s, the hardest thing about mowing the lawn was getting the lawn mower started. Even recently, I had a lawn mower where I had to pull and pull, hoping the thing would start. The work is supposed to be mowing the lawn, not starting the mower.

The insight: we don't like it when lawn mowers don't start. And they are known for not starting. This was not a challenging insight to uncover. You can imagine the innovation team at Toro looking at their customer insights.

"What do people hate about lawn mowers?"

"When they won't start."

"What if we had a lawn mower that always started? What if we could *guarantee* that it would start?"

"Well, how would we do that?"

They set about creating a lawn mower that would always start—a worthy undertaking. Then they launched the Guaranteed to Start campaign. I own a Toro lawn mower, and sure enough, every time I pull the cord, it starts.

Midas has a powerful Because: "Because we will guarantee it for as long as you own your car."

LifeLock has a powerful Because: "Because we will back you up with $1 million in coverage for lawyers and experts."

Toro has a powerful Because: "Because it's guaranteed to start."

What do you guarantee? What will you say to back up your guarantee?

## 7. Novel Approach and Innovation

The way we've always done it is fine until something new and better comes along. Sometimes customers do not even know they need something better until an innovator shows them what is possible. In this case, there can be a phase of educating customers about what the new thing does and why they should care. Sometimes this requires leading customers to insights they didn't even know they had. Other times, it's taking general trends or insights and applying it to a category.

Dropps does both. Dropps sells a line of laundry products and other household cleaners. I was first introduced to Dropps by Stacey Crowley, a certified facilitator of the Because Framework. She sent me a two-minute video, featuring the CEO of Dropps, called "The Naked Truth about Laundry." Stacey said, "Watch this video. It's packed with Becauses!"

In just two minutes, the video presents ten outcomes backed by seventeen Becauses. Let's just say by the end of the video, I was convinced and became a customer. In the video, Jonathan Propper, the CEO, promises outcomes based on insights like the desire for clean laundry, saving money, and being eco-friendly. Watching him list all their Becauses is a humorous part of the video. It even includes one of the most compelling Becauses in text that goes by so quickly you have to freeze the video to read it—a very creative way to get customers to engage with the video. The video also does a great job establishing the personality of the CEO and the brand. He's funny and engaging. The drama draws you in and is related to the Becauses. Want to see how many Becauses you can pack in two minutes? Visit **TheyBuyYourBecause .com** to see "The Naked Truth about Laundry."

What are you doing today that is new and different from how it's been done in the past?

## Try Them All

There are many ways to create Becauses for your company, your product, or your service. What proof can you use to finish the sentence of influence? Try to innovate around each of the Because approaches. Some of them will work for you better than others, but each will challenge your thinking about creating or demonstrating proof to your customers.

Here is a quick review of the seventeen Because techniques:

### Systematic Proof
1. Proprietary Processes, Systems, or Methodologies
2. Proprietary Technology
3. Unique Formulations, Ingredients, or Materials
4. Quality Substantiation, Testing Process, or Certifications

### Perceived Proof
1. Specialization
2. Size
3. Statistics and Track Record
4. Social Proof
5. Visual Proof
6. Third-Party Credibility

### Created Proof
1. Product and Service Differentiators
2. Pricing Structure
3. Customization
4. Extra Value
5. Unique Company Structure
6. Guarantee
7. Novel Approach and Innovation

Who are your ideal customers, what insights do you have about them, what outcome do you promise, and what are your Becauses? Answer these questions, complete your sentence of influence, and close the sale.

# PART IV

# THE BECAUSE FRAMEWORK

## Three Actions to Innovate and Implement Your Becauses

# Innovate

W HAT DO you do if you don't have any powerful
Becauses? In my experience, this is rare. However,
this was basically the situation of the whole light
beer industry in the mid-2000s when I became brand manager of Coors Light. If you don't have powerful Becauses,
it's time to innovate. Focus your innovation around creating
Becauses that are valuable to your customers, unique to you,
and hard to copy.

Even if you have many Becauses, you must constantly
innovate to maintain distance between you and your competitors. The Because Framework is the foundation for innovation.
*Who* are you targeting, what are their *insights*, what is the *outcome* you promise, and what's your *Because*?

Netflix bankrupted the multibillion-dollar Blockbuster
Video brand. But they didn't stop there. While Netflix initially made its mark by mailing DVDs, it soon transitioned to
streaming, mostly obsoleting its own DVD business model.

That, in turn, disrupted internet service providers when
Netflix streaming began to eat up lots of their bandwidth. By
2015, Netflix accounted for over 36 percent of all the peak

period downstream internet traffic in North America.[1] Netflix, along with other internet companies, fought the cable providers to preserve net neutrality, preventing the providers from slowing download speeds for companies like Netflix.

The next major innovation from Netflix was creating its own content. What are the *insights* about watching TV shows? What do TV viewers want more of and less of in their viewing? They do not like commercials, and they do not like that they have to wait for each episode to be released.

So, when Netflix launched its own shows, it released an entire season all at once. No more waiting week after week for your show to come on. And, of course, on Netflix there were no advertisements to disrupt your viewing. More of what you want and less of what you don't. It created a whole new phenomenon called binge watching. Netflix now produces its own series and movies. They have huge A-list stars and massive production budgets. Netflix is now a major player in Hollywood.

Netflix went from disrupting Blockbuster to innovating streaming, disrupting internet service providers, disrupting television, and then disrupting Hollywood altogether. It has broken several long-standing models based on simple but powerful customer insights. But as is always the case, competitors have flooded into the space trying to steal Netflix's customers. When you are an innovative leader, your competitors are sure to follow. That's why the best companies are constantly listening to their customers and driving innovation. Using the Because Framework is not an endgame; it's a journey.

How will you innovate your company and your *industry*?

While you are working through the Because Framework, new, innovative ideas will emerge all along the way. Be sure to capture those ideas so you can evaluate and work on them later. One of them could change your future.

# Using the Because Framework is not an endgame. It's a journey.

Innovation improves your product or service so it provides more *value* to your customers. The companies that thrive over time are continually innovating. They are always listening to their customers, watching their competitors, and navigating their way to what's next. The best companies are in a constant state of iterative learning. They try something, evaluate the results, then keep it, kill it, or improve it. Focus your innovation efforts on creating valuable differentiation that is hard for your competitors to copy.

Today, consumers *expect* innovation from your company. They expect what you deliver tomorrow to be superior to what you are delivering today. Think about apps on your phone. Your expectation is that next month or next quarter, each app will be updated to function better and add more value to your life. It is no longer sufficient to continually deliver the status quo to your customers. They are accustomed to receiving constant, ongoing upgrades. How have you recently upgraded your product, service, or customer experience?

## Innovation Starts with Insights

Innovation comes from insights. Use the Because Framework to gain a clear understanding of your customers and their insights. When you do, new ideas and innovation will bubble up from every part of your organization. The framework enables every team member to think of innovative ways to deliver new value to your customers.

Use your customer insights as a challenge to your team. Use the following list of "What if…" statements to initiate discussion and brainstorming. Look at your insights and ask:

- What if we…
- What if we solved…
- What if we delivered…
- What if we expanded…
- What if we eliminated…
- What if we pursued…
- What if we created…
- What if we challenged…
- What if we proved…
- What if we discovered…
- What if we patented…
- What if we changed…
- What if we communicated…
- What if we initiated…
- What if we reduced…
- What if we promised…

Sometimes challenges that don't seem possible become possible when you focus on them. How would your business change if you were able to address your customers' problems, frustrations, hopes, and fears in a new way?

During your ideation, focus on which of the insights lead to innovations and ideas that also deliver valuable outcomes and create powerful Becauses. Create innovations that demonstrate and prove the unique value you will deliver to your customers. Involve everyone in your organization in innovation. Institute mechanisms to encourage constant collection of insights, innovative ideas, and valuable improvements for your customers. Create rewards for innovative ideas, and bigger rewards for those that ultimately get implemented.

## Difficult Is Better

Difficult innovation is harder for competitors to copy. What would be a challenge for you but valuable for your customers? What could you do that your competitors are unwilling to do, unable to do, or haven't done?

> ## Things that are hard to do are also hard to copy.

What innovation would allow you to say "We are the only..."? "We show up at a specific time, not in a four-hour window." "We sell you a car for one price, from one person, in one hour." "All our calls are answered by the third ring by a live person." Things that are hard to do are also hard to copy. If it's easy, your competitors can copy you quickly. If it's difficult, you'll have some runway.

Innovation can help make your problem your solution. How do you make your limitation your advantage? Let's say you're an HVAC company that serves wealthy neighborhoods. The only repair techs available to hire are young and new to the industry. Older customers might not believe that young repair techs have the experience to repair their furnace or air conditioner. How can you innovate your message so this becomes your advantage?

Would you rather have a young person who goes to factory training four times a year fixing your furnace or an older tech who's been doing it forever the same way it was done twenty years ago? What about putting in that new internet-connected thermostat that you can voice activate and talks to your phone? Who do you trust more to do that? The older tech or the younger? What Becauses can you create so homeowners trust your techs regardless of age? "Because every one of our techs is factory certified on both the oldest and newest technologies."

## Every Company Can Innovate

Any industry and any company can leverage innovation. If you don't innovate your industry, someone else will. Whether your industry is B to B or B to C, glamorous or plain, large or small, innovation can be created. Has there been much recent innovation in your industry? If not, there may be opportunity. Consider the brilliant innovation by Bob Robinson, the founder of Kaivac.

Picture this. Your job is to clean restrooms. In a sports stadium. Hmm. Bummer. Why don't you want your job to be cleaning restrooms? Well, it's probably smelly, dirty, and frankly challenging. You must scrub and clean and wipe in lots of dirty, wet, sticky places. No fun, and no one is probably that excited about it.

What if you oversaw a big restroom cleaning crew? Do you suppose your turnover might be high? Do you suppose hiring might be a challenge? Do you suppose your team motivation could be low? Do you suppose your quality control could be a problem? These are your *insights*.

## If you don't innovate your industry, someone else will.

What if there was a cleaning equipment company that could solve your biggest employee and quality challenges? A company that had innovated a whole different approach. What if there was a cleaning technology that focused on the insights of the workers *doing* the cleaning? What if that company eliminated the undesirable parts of cleaning, increased quality and employee retention, and made it more fun all at the same time?

Sometimes in life I come across a product that is so ingenious that I believe everyone should be buying it. This is one of those products. It's called the Kaivac No-Touch Cleaning system. In 1997 the founder of Kaivac, Bob Robinson, set out to develop a more dignified and more productive method of cleaning restrooms. His innovation was a brand-new approach to restroom cleaning that is faster, more effective, and frankly looks like a lot more fun. Instead of mopping, wiping, and scrubbing toilets, Kaivac sells a system that sprays everything down with a cleaning solution and then vacuums it all up. No touching anything. Every surface is cleaned and dried with no touching. And it's kind of fun, right?

They back up their innovation with all sorts of statistics that prove how effective it is. Kaivac has delivered on every insight of restroom cleaners and the companies they work for. I think it's useful to read their own words to see the power of their Becauses in action. You have to love this language: "The public restroom is essentially a biohazardous waste transfer station."

Look for their insights, outcomes (promises), and Becauses (proof). They're all there. Here is the content right from their website:

*A High-Risk Environment*
There's no denying, restroom cleaning is the number one building maintenance concern. Restrooms are also probably the number one building health hazard too. That's because the public restroom is essentially a biohazardous waste transfer station—a primary source of bacteria within a building...

*The Problem with Mops*
Traditional tools, such as mops and wipes, do a poor job of removing soils, bacteria, and other contaminants and are tedious to use. Kaivac's restroom cleaning systems are designed to thoroughly remove these contaminants to eliminate odors and reduce the risk of disease for the safest, healthiest results. In fact, Kaivac's restroom cleaning machines are proven to be 60 times more effective at removing bacterial contamination than mops, which are more likely to spread diseases than remove them.

*Don't Just Clean It, Kaivac It*
Kaivac's systems not only clean better, but also cut labor, chemical, and equipment costs while raising worker morale and image. Kaivac's restroom cleaning machines combine automatic chemical metering and injection, an indoor pressure washer, and a powerful wet vacuum into a single integrated system. The chemical metering ensures accurate dilution and a savings of up to 90 percent.

Productivity is dramatically increased compared to conventional cleaning methods. According to ISSA, it takes an average of three minutes to clean a restroom fixture. In many restrooms, Kaivac's systems cut that time to one minute, leaving surfaces sparkling clean in one-third the time. Plus, workers are no longer forced to crawl around restroom floors, wiping fixtures and surfaces by hand... Regardless of stature or physical ability, Kaivac's restroom cleaning equipment allows workers to deep clean surfaces and fixtures, while producing the same healthy results every time.

Kaivac started with *insights* of restroom cleaners and the companies they work for. They created a new-to-the-world innovation that delivers valuable *outcomes* to their customers, and they back it up with many powerful *Becauses*. How many Becauses can you find in their web content? Notice that they have used Becauses from multiple categories including statistics, proprietary technology, and third-party credibility.

The Kaivac example also demonstrates another important point. Your marketing and sales language doesn't need to be brief to be effective. Different situations call for different-length explanations. Different mediums, individuals, and stages in the sales flow will all impact how much time you have to make your case. You can imagine that Kaivac has short, medium, and long versions of this for use in different situations.

## Innovating a Commodity

I've worked with several companies and industries that produce or distribute commodities—oil and gas, steel, and chemicals, for example.

The products themselves may be commodities, but the companies are not. Regularly, the commodity companies that are thriving are delivering value that is *different* from competitors and *valuable* to their customers. Many times, these value-added factors have been developed at a great cost to the company.

Sometimes, they deliver consultative expertise. Their industry knowledge helps them help their customers by providing ideas, education, and perspective. Sometimes they provide industry information, research, or benchmarking. Sometimes they provide better service through more extensive inventories or a wider selection of specific products. Sometimes they provide frontline training, technology, and tools to their customers. If your product is a commodity, your value comes from everything that surrounds it. You may sell commodities, but a commodity you are not.

## You may sell commodities, but a commodity you are not.

Even commodities themselves have a long history of being innovated. A century-old example of delivering a valuable new outcome in a commodity is Morton Salt. Salt is literally a commodity. You might remember this from high school chemistry class: it's a chemical compound—NaCl. The problem with salt is that in humid conditions, it cakes together and doesn't flow freely. In 1911, Morton devised a process to add an anticaking agent to table salt, allowing it to flow freely. This ultimately led to the creation of their famous tagline "When It Rains, It Pours"—literally meaning when the salt gets humid, it still pours.

This was a big benefit for salt at the time. They later introduced the well-known round blue container. This also had added benefits. The container was made with a moisture-resistant top and bottom and a moisture-proof liner. Morton Salt now has a huge market share of all the salt in the world.

## The Because Innovation Process

If salt, beer, and bathroom cleaning can be innovated, so can your industry. The Because Innovation Process is a simple framework you can follow to apply the Because principles to your innovation. The process of innovation is focused on creating new Becauses. You leverage insights from your customers to generate new products, processes, and proof that you are the best choice for your customers. You create new ways to solve your customers' problems better than any of your competitors.

The first four steps of the because Innovation Process are the Core Four Questions you've already learned. I've included a summary of each for easy reference. Then there are five more steps to create and implement your innovations.

### 1. Identify Your Ideal Customers

You may sell to many different customer types, but since the foundation of all innovation is customer insights, it's valuable to focus on each customer type individually as you undertake innovation brainstorming. The smaller the sandbox, the bigger the creativity. Get specific about who you are serving, and you will experience the power of specificity in generating insights and ideas. You can run the process again and again for different customer types and even for employees.

## 2. Gather Insights

The most important insights come from your *customers*. What do your customers want more of or less of? What do they hope for or fear? What problems are they solving, and what are their current beliefs? What are your *competitors* doing and saying? What is happening in your *industry*? What trends are important to consider? Scan the market, study your competitors, and listen to your customers. Narrow your list of key insights to between five and ten. Of those, determine which are credibly taken by competitors. Where is there space to compete?

## 3. Turn Insights into Outcomes

Your outcomes come directly from your insights. Ideally, focus your attention on outcomes that you can deliver effectively and are not credibly covered by your competitors. If your customers want to save time, the outcome you promise is time savings. If they want durability, you promise durability. If they want cold beer, promise your beer will be the coldest. Creating an outcome is simply the process of converting your top insights into the commitment you will promise. Then you prove the outcome with Becauses. This is where the Because Innovation Process delivers ideas and innovations that drive results.

## 4. Create Becauses

What will you innovate or create to prove that you will deliver your outcome? To create your Becauses, dig deep into each of the outcomes you created. Which can you credibly prove using one of the Because creation techniques? Sometimes one outcome will have many Becauses, and sometimes many outcomes will all be supported by one Because. This is the messy part of creation. Don't get frustrated: messy is okay.

## 5. Create Concepts

Create *concepts* based on your brainstorming. Turn each idea into a concept by describing who it is for (ideal customer), what problem it solves (outcome), and how it works (Because). Your concept is a succinct description of the big idea. Write it such that you could put it in front of your customers to get feedback. Each concept should include an initial assessment of its upside, complexity, investment, and timeline to execute it.

## 6. Collect Feedback

Customer feedback is a critical part of the Because Innovation Process. You may think you have created brilliant concepts, but customers with money are the final arbiters of your success. You can create a list of ten, one hundred, or one thousand innovations that you *could* execute. But which ones *should* you execute? Which ideas are easy and inexpensive to create and roll out? Which will take longer and are more expensive but are big, game-changing ideas? Of course, if you can come up with low-cost, easy ideas that are game changers, that is great. Unfortunately, in highly competitive industries, those things are hard to find.

Customer feedback will help you navigate which of your concepts to prioritize. Put your concepts in front of customers (ideally current customers, prospects, and past customers) and let them give you their opinions. You can do it in small groups, by surveys, or on social media. Any input is valuable. Have them help you think through ways to improve your concepts. Have them rank and order your concepts so you have insights about which ones are worth pursuing. Customer input can help you refine, expand, improve, fix, eliminate, and create new ideas. The process to get feedback is the same as the one you used to uncover your insights. Review the techniques in Step 2: What Are Your Insights?

### 7. Develop Projects and Teams

After you have narrowed your list of concepts, pick the ones with the most potential—the ones that have the most value for your customers and the most upside for you.

Create an *innovation leadership team* that will sponsor the projects. The leadership team is responsible for providing the resources needed to fund and staff the projects. They are also the team who ultimately decides which projects will continue to move forward and which will be stopped.

Create *project teams* with a single leader. Your project could be a product, service, process, formulation, guarantee, or anything that delivers a new and valuable outcome and Because for your customers. The project team leaders are responsible for establishing the projects and making recommendations to the innovation leadership team.

### 8. Test and Improve

I have worked on innovations at Procter & Gamble, Coors, Quiznos, and Red Robin. Innovation is messy. Testing and iteration are critical parts of the process that many companies skip. Do not skip these steps.

Your product or service will improve with testing and iteration. The key is to iterate quickly based on what you learn from testing. Learn, make changes, test again. Your initial innovation doesn't have to be perfect. It is much more effective to get it out in the world, sell some of it, and get feedback rather than trying to make it perfect right out of the gate.

Failure is part of innovation. Not everything works, and not all the ideas are winners. That is okay. Eliminate the failures as fast as possible, and focus on the ideas that produce results. Great businesses are grown through navigating. Invest in what works, and stop what doesn't.

## 9. Launch

If you've done your innovation work well, you've created compelling differentiated Becauses. They only make a difference in your business when you launch the initiative and close some sales. Create a launch plan that includes:

- **Because Platform:** What are your key insights, outcomes, and Becauses?

- **Launch leader:** Who's responsible? Assign one point person.

- **Target lists:** Include current customers and new prospects that will benefit from this innovation.

- **Sales launch responsibility:** Who will get this innovation in front of your ideal customers and when?

- **Marketing launch responsibility:** Who will create and execute the marketing and sales tools, and where will they be deployed?

- **Launch calendar:** When is everything happening, and who is on point?

- **Operational support:** Who else in the organization needs to be involved to ensure sales, marketing, and customers get the support they need for success?

- **Goals:** What specifically do you hope to achieve and by when? What impact will this have on the company?

- **Measures:** How will you measure your success?

## Because Innovation Summit

One way to jumpstart innovation is to hold a Because Innovation Summit. During the summit, everyone in your organization spends a day brainstorming innovative ideas.

I led a Because Innovation Summit for Level Legal, a legal services firm with over one hundred attorneys and support staff in attendance. Many important initiatives were established in a single day, and it instituted a culture of innovation in every part of the firm.

A couple weeks before the summit, the entire company attended my keynote presentation inspiring them about innovation and the power of Because. Then each of them submitted ideas to improve the company.

On the day of the summit, self-selected teams went to work on eleven of the most popular ideas. The session set the company on a new path. It not only created game-changing innovations for the firm; it was a cultural transformation. Everyone was involved, had the chance to be heard, and learned that their voice and ideas matter. The summit created a structure for continuous ideation and an innovation mindset in the firm. Everyone contributed to where the company will go in the next five years.

When I facilitate Because Innovation Summits, ideas emerge, camaraderie increases, and employee morale is boosted. It's also a unique opportunity for executive management to watch every employee in action and see new leaders emerging. While brainstorming and creation is not everyone's forte, the best ideas many times come from where you least expect them.

What will you do to drive innovation in your company? How will you disrupt your industry before one of your competitors does? Now is your opportunity to be the leader so you don't become a follower. Take a minute to write down your top three customer frustrations and ideate innovations in your business that could solve them. Have your team do the same, and see what you put into motion.

## STEP 6

# Create Your Because Platform

YOU'VE DONE it. You have narrowed your focus to your ideal customers, gathered insights, turned those insights into outcomes, and created powerful Becauses. You've innovated, iterated, and enhanced your messages.

You may have multiple customer types, outcomes, and Becauses. You likely have created so much that you feel overwhelmed by the volume of your ideas. What's next? How do you put it to work in your company?

One of the top questions I receive from companies implementing the Because Framework is whether it is okay to have multiple Becauses. Absolutely. You may have multiple customer types, numerous insights, and many outcomes and Becauses. The key is to organize all of these into useful tools for your company so you can put them to work where and when they matter.

Whenever you have a question, refer back to the Framework. Who are you trying to influence right now? What are their insights? What is the outcome you promise to deliver? And what is your proof—your Because?

## The Because Platform

After using the Because Framework to uncover insights and to create outcomes and Becauses, the next step is to create your Because Platform. The Framework is the *process* and the Platform is the *road map*. It is how you insert your Becauses at each of the critical influence points. Your Because Platform is made up of your Influence Statements (text or visual), your Because Map, your Because Matrix, your selling tools, and your sales flow. These tools help you insert your messages at the right place at the right time to close sales.

Depending on your business, there may be many different individuals you need to influence at different times in your sales process. Most businesses I work with are complex businesses with long sales cycles. Customer interactions and decision-making processes can be complicated with multiple influence points along the journey.

For each customer type, individual, or influence point, the Because Framework can be used to maximize your results. The Framework should become part of the fabric of your company, your innovation, and your decision-making process. The Because Platform you create should be integrated into your sales process, your marketing, your proposals, and everything else you do to communicate your value proposition to customers.

## Influence Statements

Create *Influence Statements* to hone and refine your ideas. Influence Statements combine your insights, outcomes, and Becauses into conceptual statements. They are *sentences of influence.* They describe a proposition that is unique to you and valuable to your customers. They are clear, succinct statements about what business you are in, *who* you serve, *what* value you promise to deliver, and the *proof* that you will deliver. They are the first step in turning your brainstorming into actionable messages that will influence your customers.

The process of creating Influence Statements is messy. Many of us are uncomfortable with the messiness of creation, but that is where the magic happens. Have everyone on the team create several Influence Statements that include your top customer insights, outcomes, and Becauses. Work individually to craft the most compelling way to describe your ideas. Then share your statements across the team. Comment on which ideas and language stands out. Mix, match, and combine ideas. Steal each other's best work to create the most powerful concepts possible.

You will begin to hear things that sound powerful and things that sound like marketing fluff. The creative process helps the best ideas to float to the top. Your ear, your gut, and your subconscious will know which things will be the most compelling to your customers and which will fall flat.

### Influence Statement Structure

The format below is the foundation for creating Influence Statements. It is a good starting point, but as you create your statements, you can expand, modify, and rearrange them as long as they include the key components—ideal customer, outcome, Because. The order doesn't matter as long as you deliver your idea in a clear, compelling way.

### Influence Statement

For [insert **Customer** here],

[insert **Business Name** here] is the

[insert **Category** here] that provides

[insert **Outcome** here].

That's because [insert **Becauses** here].

### Examples

For  twenty-one- to twenty-four-year-old men ,

Coors Light  is the

light beer  that provides

cold refreshment .

That's because  every can has a blue liner that locks in refreshing frost-brewed taste .

For  _restroom cleaning companies_ ,

_Kaivac_  is the

_cleaning system_  that provides

_cleaner restrooms faster, with happier cleaning personnel_ .

That's because  _only Kaivac has the patented No-Touch_
_Cleaning system that is 60 times more effective at remov-_
_ing bacterial contamination than mops, increases employee_
_morale, and reduces chemical costs by up to 90 percent_ .

For  _people frustrated with_
_the runaround at car dealerships_ ,

_Schomp_  is the

_dealer_  that has created

_a hassle-free car buying experience_ .

That's because  _at Schomp you can buy a car for one price,_
_from one person, in one hour. No haggling, no runaround,_
_no wasting your day_ .

Be succinct. While you are creating your initial statements, try to include only one customer, one outcome, and
as many Becauses as you can. This is a disciplined way to draft
ideas as you're in creation mode. You can always combine
ideas into broader concepts later. You will use all your best
Influence Statements to create your Because Map and your
Because Matrix.

Some of my clients get caught up in doing the process
"right." What this framework provides is a structured way for
you to create stronger, more powerful messages and innovations for your business. Don't worry about doing the process
right. Sometimes creation fits into nice boxes; sometimes it

does not. You will likely notice that some of your Becauses support multiple outcomes. The goal is to create compelling *concepts* that will draw customers to your business by describing how you are different from your competitors in ways that customers will pay for.

### Visual Brainstorming

Many companies struggle when writing Influence Statements, mostly because they focus on finding the perfect words. A useful exercise to streamline the process is to brainstorm your Becauses visually.

Start with a circle in the middle of a page and write your outcome. Then draw nodes from your outcome listing each Because that proves you can deliver the outcome. This exercise helps you focus on uncovering all the proof for each outcome without worrying about the words. You can use this exercise in place of a text-based Influence Statement.

After leading hundreds of Because Workshops, I've found that this approach helps teams get out of the trap of trying to find the perfect language and on to creating big ideas. The concepts matter much more than the words.

Sometimes clients initially think their outcomes sound like a Because or vice versa. For example, Schomp's Because might sound like an outcome. Because you can buy a car for one price, from one person, in one hour. Technically, the outcomes are no haggle, no runaround, and time savings, and the Becauses are one price, one person, one hour. Don't worry if it's messy; focus on providing the proof that you'll deliver what you say you will.

## Visual Brainstorming

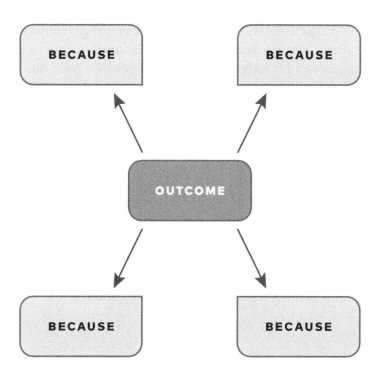

## Because Map

Your Because Map brings together all your outcomes and Becauses for a particular customer in a succinct, visual road map. It's a map outlining everything you promise (based on their insights) and how you prove that you will deliver those things better or differently than anyone else.

One large electrical contractor threw away their traditional "capabilities presentation" they used for customer meetings and replaced it with a Because Map they called their "place mat." In the center of the place mat, it simply said "You should select [name] BECAUSE..." and around that statement it outlined their eight top outcomes and related Becauses. They used it in a pitch for a $20 million electrical contract and landed the deal. They laughed after the meeting because the client had nowhere to look other than at them or at their proof they were better.

You can create a Because Map for each of your customer types. Laying out your outcomes and Becauses visually is a great way to gain alignment across the organization and gather feedback from your customers. It's also useful as you start to deploy your Becauses across every touchpoint.

## Because Map

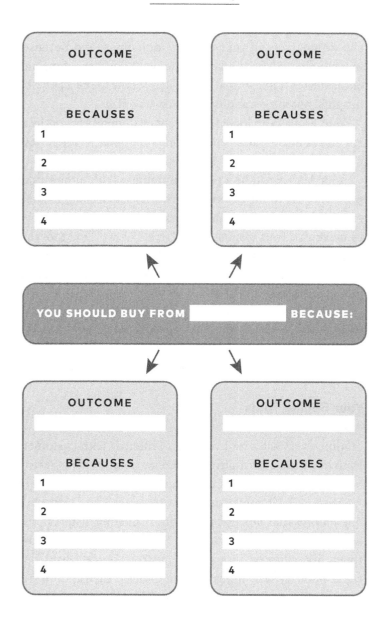

## Because Matrix

The Because Matrix is a one-page working tool that visually summarizes all your insights, outcomes, and Becauses in a simple matrix. It takes all the work you have done and encapsulates it in a format that makes it easy to see all the top insights, outcomes, and Becauses in one place.

Your Matrix can include different customer types or different stages of the sales process—anything that will help your organization understand what to say to whom and when.

Your Matrix can be a powerful training tool for new sales professionals to hit the ground running. It will align everyone in the organization about what to say and when to say it to maximize your results. The Matrix is a working tool that can be updated, changed, and improved as you learn which messages work best for which customers at which phases in the sales process.

Create your Because Matrix outline. Will yours focus on your customer types, the different individuals you influence in your sales flow, or something else?

## Your Selling Tools

Outline every sales tool you use to interact with customers. Each likely includes multiple influence points. Your objective is to insert your outcomes and Becauses at each influence point.

Most every company has sales tools such as a website, a one-on-one sales process, proposals, marketing materials, videos, and informal conversations. Some companies also have things like online reviews, a social media presence, advertising, trade publications, industry conferences, distribution networks, customer word of mouth, and many, many others.

# Because Matrix

| | Customer #1 | | Customer #2 | | Customer #3 | |
|---|---|---|---|---|---|---|
| | Outcome | Because | Outcome | Because | Outcome | Because |
| Key Message #1 | | | | | | |
| Key Message #2 | | | | | | |
| Key Message #3 | | | | | | |
| Key Message #4 | | | | | | |
| Key Message #5 | | | | | | |
| Key Message #6 | | | | | | |

Create a master list of all your sales tools. Then, gather all the materials and messages used in your marketing and sales flow. Using the Because Framework, evaluate the messaging. How does your current messaging compare with the work that you've done with the Because Framework?

Who oversees each of your messaging platforms and customer touchpoints? Many times, in an organization there are multiple people in multiple departments in charge of different sales tools. One of the benefits of using the Because Framework is that it drives alignment. It will help marketing and sales work collaboratively to create the most effective materials and messaging for the company. It can help incorporate all your departments in the marketing and sales process, so everyone is customer focused.

## The Because Framework will help marketing and sales work collaboratively.

Create a plan and a timeline for implementing your Because Framework in every customer touchpoint. Assign an individual to be responsible for each sales tool and a date when implementation will be completed. Unless someone is in charge and held to a timeline, then no one is in charge, and it will likely never happen.

## Taglines

Your Influence Statements and Because concepts are not meant to be taglines. Sometimes I've heard executives say that they are excited to use the Because Framework to come up with their new tagline. Taglines are nice, but they generally don't do much for closing the sale or generating significant revenue. Most taglines do not actually influence customers to buy from you. The reason is that they usually don't finish the sentence of influence.

## Most taglines do not actually influence customers to buy from you.

There is only one kind of tagline that even has a chance to produce results for you. It is a tagline that describes both *what* you do and your *Because* in one short, simple statement.

I'll give you an example. One of the most memorable taglines I have ever seen was at a burrito shop near the University of Wisconsin in Madison, where I completed my undergraduate degree. The burrito shop is called La Bamba and their tagline is "Burritos as big as your head." Note that their tagline describes both what they do and their Because. We serve burritos, and you should eat at La Bamba because the burritos are huge! Another example discussed earlier is Papa Johns— "Better Ingredients, Better Pizza." An outcome and a Because in just four words.

Do you have a tagline? Does your tagline talk about what you do and include a Because? If not, it's okay, but it's unlikely that it is making a significant difference in your sales. Don't worry about it. You can spend a lot of time and effort and potentially a lot of money to come up with a tagline that doesn't really do much. You are far better off to spend your time working through the Because Framework and implementing your Influence Statements in every part of your sales process. That's where revenue is built and profit is made.

## Your Sales Flow

All your touchpoints result in some kind of sales flow—possibly multiple flows. Where do your clients first learn about you, and what journey do they take between there and becoming your client or customer? Take the time to diagram your sales flow. What are all the stages and touchpoints that happen from the beginning to the end? This is a great team exercise.

During a two-day Because Workshop with a sales team, I asked them if they had a sales flow. The first response was "Of course we do." After some debate and discussion, it turned out that individually they had their own ideas about what the flow was, but as an organization they really had no consistent understanding of the customer journey. Two hours later, they had diagrammed their sales flow. Then we got to work plugging their Becauses into the flow.

When I was working with the law firm Ciancio Ciancio Brown, we diagrammed their sales process. Their process normally starts with either a referral or a visit to their website. Then it turns into a phone call, which is received by the intake person. At that point, the client is evaluated and referred to one of several attorneys within the firm. Then the sales process proceeds from there.

# Sales Flow

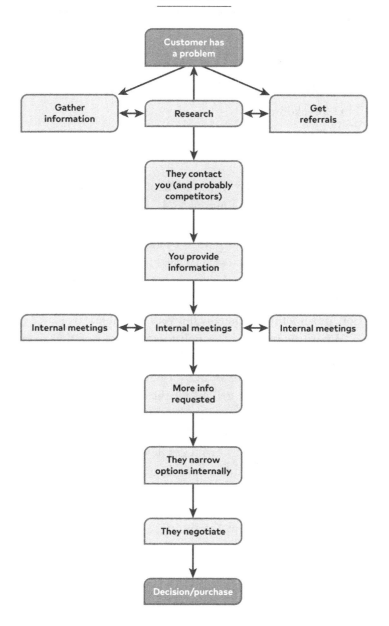

At each phase of the customer journey, there may be different insights. For the law firm, the phases unfolded as follows:

- Research phase
- Information gathering phase (initial phone calls)
- Learning phase (talking with each firm)
- Breakdown
- Comparison and evaluation phase
- Decision

You might wonder what the breakdown phase is. As we diagrammed the sales flow, we looked at the phases from the standpoint of the customer as well as the company. We evaluated the customer insights at each step along the journey. Ciancio Ciancio Brown specializes in litigation. Their clients are often going through an incredibly stressful time in their life because they are facing criminal litigation, divorce litigation, or something generally not very desirable.

What was revealed through this process was that many times there was a phase where the clients would have an emotional breakdown. This is an overwhelming time for clients, and it's an important insight for the lawyers to understand. Navigating this emotional time can make or break the client's decision to choose one law firm vs. another.

Your company has its own sales flow with your own phases, decision-makers, and decision points. If your sales process involves a long sales cycle that happens through multiple stages or involves multiple stakeholders, take the time to diagram the exact flow, the timing, and all influence points. Diagram your customer interaction process all the way from the point that they learn about you until the time that you sign the contract or make the sale.

For example, you may be initially contacted by procurement but end up in front of operations, engineering, the CFO, and eventually the CEO. Each of these stakeholders will have different insights and care about different things. Along the way, they will be having meetings about you without you in the room. Will your prospects remember your Becauses and be able to repeat them? Will they still find them compelling when you are not there?

Who is involved in each phase of the process, and what are their insights? What outcomes do you promise, and what are your Becauses at every point? How many different customer journeys do you have? Diagram each of these so everyone in your organization understands how to maximize influence at every touchpoint.

## Customer Input

Just as you got customer input when you were gathering your insights and creating innovation, it's important to get customer feedback as you create Influence Statements, your Because Map, and your Because Matrix.

First, have an internal dialogue and debate about which concepts sound most compelling to you, then get customer feedback. Maybe you have ten Because concepts. Which of them sound the most compelling to your customers? Which of them are based on your top customer insights? Which of them deliver the most value from the customer's perspective? We can all make guesses, but the only way to know for sure is to put the statements in front of your customers and see which of them resonate.

This is a great way to build deeper and stronger relationships with customers. Ask if they would be willing to give you their opinions about your ideas to deliver more value to them moving forward. Your best customers will be excited to listen and help.

You can use techniques like one-on-one conversations, surveys, and a customer advisory panel to get feedback. You may have ten customers, one hundred customers, one thousand customers, or one million customers. Regardless, there are simple ways to put your ideas in front of them. The insights you uncover can be invaluable. Put your ideas out there and let them respond. The process to get feedback on your Because Framework is the same as the one in step 2.

## Prioritization of Communication

After using the Because Framework, you may have so many compelling Becauses you want to say them all at once. As you can imagine, that simply doesn't work. Your sales flow is made up of many influence points. Whether it's your website, your video, or your proposal, people can only process so much in a short period. So how do you prioritize your communication?

Let's use your website, for example. Who is coming to your website? What do they want to accomplish when they get there? If you only have a few seconds with your visitor, what do you want them to see first, second, and third? What journey do you want them to take so they arrive at the right conclusion (that you are the best option for them) as fast as possible? What order of communication will demonstrate that you understand their insights, can deliver the outcome they want, and have proof—your Because? Review your current website. When you open it, what is your first message, second message, and third message? What is the customer journey? How influential have you been?

Use this process for all your selling tools. Elevate your best outcomes and Becauses to be front and center. Prioritize your communication. Take your customers on a purposeful journey based on their insights. Along the journey insert your outcomes and Becauses where they matter the most. Prioritize your messages everywhere in your sales flow. Evaluate all your influence points. Use the Matrix to be sure you are optimizing your priority of communication.

## Video

Are you using video in your sales process? You should be. Today, the question is not whether you should be using video; the question is what you should say in your video to help you close sales. Using the Because Framework, you have created your key messages. Prioritize your insights, outcomes, and Becauses to create the foundation of your video script. Organize those inputs in a flow that engages the viewer, shows you understand their insights, promises outcomes, and supports them with Becauses. Videos based on your Becauses can be used in many places in your marketing plan and sales flow, including your website, your one-on-one sales conversations, your recruiting, your conference booth, your social media, and your email marketing.

You will see Becauses used in television commercials made by billion-dollar brands. Those brands consistently show the insights, promise an outcome, and deliver a powerful Because. Watch closely the next time you see a commercial, and you will find their Because.

## They Buy Your Because

Regardless of the kind of marketing, advertising, or selling you are doing, the Because Framework will enhance your efforts. Start with your customer *insights*, deliver your promise in an *outcome*, and prove it with your *Because*. Use the Framework to enhance every one of your influence points. Train everyone in your organization to understand your insights, outcomes, and Becauses. Keep them on the lookout for innovations and new ideas to create powerful Becauses that distance you from your competitors.

## STEP 7

Execute at Every
Touchpoint

LL YOUR work only matters if you actually execute on it. One of my favorite activities at the end of an in-company session is listing all the action items and then getting out a fat red marker to assign people's names to each commitment. That's when it gets real. Everyone in your organization already has a full-time job. They didn't have extra time before you did this work. Setting accountability and dates is critical. But what will they stop doing so they can do this new work? What additional resources are needed to execute your new ideas and plan? Piling more on top of an already stretched executive team will not work. Work as a team to align on priorities for the organization.

The Because Framework is designed to be deployed in every phase of your marketing and sales processes. This takes time and effort. It will be worth it, but you also need to keep up with everything it takes to run a business.

Take all the Because tools you created in step 6 and put them to work. Who do you need to influence, when, and where during every part of your sales journey? What tools and messages will you use to influence customers? Where do you think the upside exists in your company? Is it with existing customers or new customers? What are the challenges and sticking points in your sales process? Which tools in your sales flow are strong or weak? Where are you running up against walls? Where are you winning in the market against your competition? All of these factors help determine where to focus your efforts.

## Are You the Disruptor or the Disrupted?

Every industry is undergoing disruption. Much disruption is out of your control. And I'm not just talking about the pandemic. Industries are constantly going through changes in technology, economic conditions, workforce availability, customer expectations, competitive pressures, and a litany of other things. It's your job as a leader to navigate these disruptions so that you continue to grow, even through all the changes.

It's also your job as a leader to proactively disrupt your organization before your competitors, customers, or the world disrupts you. The first year Tiger Woods ever played professionally on the PGA tournament, 1996, he was twenty-one years old. That year, he won 25 percent of all the PGA tournaments he entered, an amazing win rate for a twenty-one-year-old golfer.[1] By 1998, he only won 5 percent. Why? Because he changed his swing. He disrupted himself. Disruption is messy, but as an athlete, or as a company, sometimes you need to get messy in order to get stronger. By 2000, he won 45 percent of the tournaments he entered. Then he plateaued. In 2004, he changed his swing again, and in 2008, he won 67 percent of his tournaments.

## Tiger Woods Wins

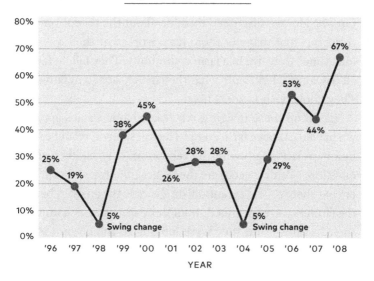

This is how you become legendary. As a leader, it's your opportunity and your responsibility to lead your organization through proactive change. Great leaders show their organizations what is possible and navigate them through disruption on the path to success. What should you be disrupting? Do you need to innovate your sales flow, your products, your marketing, or your recruiting? What disruption today will make you a stronger competitor tomorrow? Your Becauses and innovations are the foundations for proactively disrupting your company or industry.

## Breaking Through Gatekeepers

Kop-Coat, the adjuvant company discussed in the section on Systematic Proof, studied its sales flow and uncovered a sticking point. The salespeople were having a hard time breaking through gatekeepers at farm co-ops. The receptionists were all trained to say no to any salespeople who called. During our session, we discussed insights about the receptionists. It turns out that many of them have worked at the co-op for a long time. They live in a farm community. They talk to farmers all day long. They *know* what the farmers are struggling with. They know what farmers need.

Based on these insights, we created a new sales approach when cold calling a farm co-op. The salesperson would call and build a relationship with the receptionist by asking a simple question: "Which weeds are the biggest nightmare for the farmers out there?" The receptionists all knew the answer, because the farmers were frustrated about those weeds, which impacted their business, and they were looking to the co-op for help.

"Oh, we have two big ones here: pigweed and marestail. Nothing will kill those..."

"Yeah, those are tough. I'm with Kop-Coat, and we've just patented a new product that will kill both of those. Who's the person to talk to about coming out there to do a test?" With this simple flow, gatekeepers regularly passed the salesperson to the buyer.

## Find your sticking points, anticipate the objections, and head them off at the pass.

By breaking through the gatekeepers, Kop-Coat was able to have the critical conversations with decision-makers, run tests, and gain distribution. Find your sticking points, anticipate the objections, head them off at the pass, and then be sure to deliver on your commitments.

## Nobody Wants a Raisin Cookie

If you make bold promises about outcomes you'll deliver, you need to actually deliver those promises. If you say you're going to show up on time, then you need to show up. If you say your pizza is going to taste better, it had better taste good.

Have you ever been at a conference where they have a cookie break between speakers? You grab a chocolate chip cookie on your way back into the meeting, and when you sit down you realize that it wasn't a chocolate chip cookie. It was a raisin cookie! Yuck. (Yes, I know some of you like raisin cookies—there are always a few in the crowd.)

The point is not whether you like raisin or not; it's whether you got what you *thought* you were getting. If you promise a chocolate chip cookie and give a raisin cookie, your customers will be disappointed no matter how good your raisin cookie is. Make a commitment and then deliver that commitment. How will you ensure that everyone in your organization knows your customer commitments and knows their role in delivering on them? Alignment, consistency, and execution build great brands.

**Nobody wants a raisin cookie
if they thought they were
getting a chocolate chip cookie.**

## Engage and Empower Your Front Lines

I recently underwent a major renovation of my home. Hardwood flooring was an important part of the renovation. One of my designers said, "It is the most expensive piece of furniture you will ever buy." And once it's in, it's not easy to change.

I was looking for a very specific shade of flooring. I had looked at many samples and found some that were in the range of what I wanted. I picked out a beautiful sample of quality flooring, but I was concerned that I was only looking at a two-foot-by-two-foot square. I was going to be installing many, many square feet and was worried that the installed flooring wouldn't look like the sample. So I ordered a full box of the flooring to see what it really looked like.

When I laid out the box of flooring, it did not look anything like the sample. It was the correct floor, but it didn't look the same. The sample looked fresh and beautiful, and the actual floor looked drab, muddy, and sort of green. Of course, I did not buy thousands of square feet of the flooring. Thank goodness I had headed off the disaster. I didn't buy the raisin cookie.

I went back to the sales rep to say that I wanted to return the box of flooring because it didn't match the sample. He said he wasn't sure if the company would take it back. Weeks went by, and finally the answer came back that the company had determined that the sample was "within spec." I had shown the floor to ten different people, all of whom questioned why it looked so different from the sample. The factory declined to allow the return, clearly not empowering the sales rep to do the right thing by the customer.

I pointed out to the rep that I was doing the company a favor by giving them the feedback before someone would accidentally put in flooring that didn't look anything like the sample. When that happens, they are going to have a real problem, possibly a lawsuit. I honestly thought I was doing them a favor. For this favor, they just needed to restock one box of flooring. A great value, in my opinion.

The most valuable feedback you can get is from customers who are disappointed or who have chosen not to work with you. Customers willing to give you feedback are a tremendous resource if you listen to them. They can help you make your business better and stronger. Those customers can be hard to find, so when you find one, learn everything you can. If you ignore those customers just to take a little revenue, it is short-sighted and can be very risky.

How do you get the customers to talk to you? They already are talking—you just need to empower the people they are talking *to* to listen and take action. Your front lines are in the best position to listen to your customers and gain valuable insights. While you may not like what you hear, that's where the value is. Insights from customers drive innovation and are the foundation of your Becauses.

Create a listening organization where everyone is trained to listen effectively and then feed those insights back into the organization so everyone can gain value from what they learn. What systems can you use to proactively collect insights, review them, take action, and then communicate back to the front lines on your progress?

**Create a listening organization where everyone is trained to listen effectively and then feed those insights back into the organization.**

## The Add-On Sale: Delivering a Complete Experience

*Selling* has almost become a bad word in our society. Many times, front-line employees are wary to offer something extra in the moment because they don't want to seem pushy. But your customers don't want to buy from you and then later find out there was something additional they should have added or upgraded.

I recently got a car back from the shop after a major repair. They had my car for three days, and when I got the car back, I noticed that the oil change was due. It said it right there on the window sticker. I did not have time to run my car back to the shop to get the oil changed. I really wished they would have noticed and added on an oil change to my service.

This sale is simple: "Hey, would you like us to change the oil while we have your vehicle here? We did a complimentary full inspection and noticed that your sticker says it was done on this date at this many miles. We'd be happy to get it done for you."

> ## Not offering everything that the customer may want in the moment is a disservice to them.

Not offering everything that the customer may want in the moment is a disservice to them. Make sure they know what other options are available. Providing all the information will allow them to upsell themselves. That's delivering a complete experience, not being pushy.

## Following Up after the Sale:
## Preventing Buyer's Remorse

We get buyer's remorse when we make an emotional decision and our brains, gut, and subconscious can't find a logical, rational reason why it was a good call.[2] Thus, it's important that we reinforce the client's decision before, during, and after the sale. It's not enough just to deliver your outcome: your customer needs to know that you delivered it and appreciate it.

Following up after the sale is an opportunity to reinforce your Becauses. Customers want to make a good decision, and they don't want to have any question about whether that decision was the right decision. If you don't follow up after the sale, you leave open the opportunity that there was something about their experience that wasn't quite perfect. Great companies make sure that customers remember they made a good call and that they can repeat their Becauses to others.

I rented a hotel room in New York City while leading a Because Workshop there. Since I knew I'd be leading the workshop, I saved some money by prepaying for the hotel room. I got an email from Hilton saying, "Well played. You got a great deal on a room." Boy, did I feel smart. They reinforced my decision to prepay for the room. It made me feel like I had made a good call and gotten a great deal. How do you reinforce to your customers that they made a good decision?

Following up after the sale also allows you to find out what could have gone better. You can follow up with a personal one-on-one outreach, an email, a survey, a phone call, or a customer visit. The initial email from Hilton reinforced my decision, and the follow-up email after my stay asked how they did. This kind of outreach can head off dissatisfied customers from not buying again or complaining to someone else before they complain to you. The hard feedback is the most valuable, actionable feedback. Innovation comes from learning what did not go well so you can execute better next time.

Following up after the sale is also an opportunity to build your customer relationship and possibly get referrals. Many businesses generate much of their business from referrals. If you want referrals, you must ask for them. Your customers probably like you, but they are busy. Customers are typically happy to help, but if you don't ask for the referral, they may not think about it.

## Following up after the sale is an opportunity to reinforce your Becauses, build relationships, and get referrals.

For your best customers, this is also an opportunity to ask for a testimonial. Video or written testimonials are great Becauses, especially if they come from impressive or prominent clients. You won't get one if you don't ask.

You can systematize following up after the sale. Make it a consistent part of your sales process. This is an opportunity to build your relationship and listen. Creating a listening organization starts with talking to your customers, truly listening to their feedback, and taking action. If they give you ideas, follow up with them when those ideas have been considered or implemented.

Every person in your company helps create the listening organization. If you systematize the listening and follow-up process, you will be sure that every customer feels heard and important to your company.

## Communication and Organizational Alignment

As you develop Becauses, it is important to get feedback not only from your customers but also from your employees. They need to understand the Framework and how they can put it to work. Each employee should understand what they can individually do to help the company maximize its influence with customers. Usually your frontline workers have the biggest impact on your customers and will also come up with the best ideas for innovation.

Often, a company's use of the Because Framework starts at the executive level. The CEO and key executives gather in a conference room to learn the Framework and use the process to create outcomes and Becauses. But if it doesn't spread to the rest of the company, the power of the work is not maximized. Executive team leadership, understanding, and buy-in is critical but not sufficient. Engage the entire organization in the Because Framework. This allows them to understand and contribute to the work. Of course, your Becauses are important for sales and marketing. But when everyone adopts the Framework, the power of your Becauses will take hold and change the trajectory of your success.

**Executive team buy-in is critical but not sufficient. Engage the entire organization in the Because Framework.**

The other benefit of including the organization along the journey is that when you roll out the Becauses in your sales process, your website, or sales video, everyone will understand why and how they work. They will understand the Framework, the innovations, and the messages that will be used to influence customers and grow the company. Great transformation doesn't begin and end in the boardroom. Many times, it begins there but comes to life on the front lines.

## The Framework Is Complete

The Because Framework is complete. It is not easy, but it is complete. If you are running up against challenges in sales, go back to the Framework. If you are not closing the sale, either you are focused on the wrong customer, you have not uncovered the right insights, or they do not find your Becauses compelling.

There are lots of reasons why customers may not buy from you. Some of those are out of your control, and you will never overcome them. Customers really are emotional, and sometimes they'll make decisions that are suboptimal for their company or their life. Sometimes it's because of a preexisting relationship that you can't break through. Sometimes it's because of their internal compensation structures. Sometimes it's because of how they evaluate RFPs. You might not like these things, but they are all insights and present an opportunity to improve your pitch if you know what you're up against.

If you are not being successful, go back to the Framework and determine where something is missing. You can't control all the external factors, but you can use the Framework to be as influential as possible. Who are you influencing, what are your insights, what's your outcome, and what's your Because?

That truly is the structure of influence. There isn't another model, approach, or guru who is going to magically solve your sales challenges. This is not easy, but it works. Stick with it, put in the work, collaborate with your team, and someday you're going to wake up at three a.m. with a brilliant new innovation, approach, or Because to close the sale.

## What Is Possible

Over and over, I find that the companies most committed to using the Because Framework are already the most successful. There is a reason why companies pull away from the pack. They take every opportunity to learn and then execute based on what they have learned. Companies that are already successful use the Framework to get that much better.

They revisit it year after year to stay focused on customer insights, hone their outcomes, and continue to innovate new Becauses. They use it to align their organization, to ensure their messages are compelling and consistent, and to inform their annual planning.

What would it be like to live in a world where we understood every company's Becauses? Where we were certain which choice was the best? Where messages were as clear and compelling as the ones featured in this book? Since our world isn't that way, the opportunity is big for everyone who does this work. Most companies will continue to do things the way they've always done them.

If you're one of the few who is willing to narrow your focus, understand your customers' insights, promise valuable outcomes, and support them with compelling Becauses, you will win, and your customers will win with you. You will be a better option, and your customers will understand what makes you superior. They will tell others because they know what to say and whom to say it to.

**They will buy your Because.**

PLEASE REACH out to me and share your stories of implementing the Because Framework in your company.

Visit **TheyBuyYourBecause.com** to learn about implementing the Because Framework in your company. You can work with Gerry, with a certified Because facilitator, or through the online Because Workshop.

# Acknowledgments
## This Is Because of You

LIVE IN gratitude for my life every day. Nothing in my life would have been possible without the help of others. This book is the culmination of my life's journey and is my life's work. It was only possible because of the people who have contributed to that journey. Each stage of my life has built upon the previous stages in ways I never could have anticipated or imagined.

So, my acknowledgments are not about those who helped me write the book. I'm acknowledging those who helped me create my life, even the ones who are no longer here to read this.

Thank you, Mom and Dad, for a childhood that made me who I am today. I loved it and love who it has helped me become. Thank you to my brother, Bob, and sister, Mary, for sharing some of the most memorable years of my life. Our childhood was ours, and it is a treasure for me. Thank you all for being a low-drama family who enjoys one another.

Thank you to everyone in Columbus, Wisconsin, who has ever been around there in my life. It was an amazing place to grow up and call home. While I've moved away and traveled the world, my heart is still in Columbus.

Thanks to all my teachers from Columbus High School, especially Mr. Byfield for teaching life, not just classes; Mr. Zahn for giving me the platform for my first speech; Mrs. Dickman for igniting my love for literature; and Mr. Lang for teaching me to type. Who knew how important that would eventually become?

Thank you, Marc Rhode, my best friend in high school and still today. It's been a great journey for decades. Thanks for the bowling pin, the Fiat, the Violent Femmes, the dome, and one too many old-fashioneds.

Thank you, Chris Tobison, Mike McLean, and John and Doris Dingee for changing my life when you were here. Chris, you inspired me to go to college. Without you, I'm not sure where my journey would have taken me. Mike, you helped me to get out of my shell. John and Doris, you showed me what is possible and how to be a gentleman.

Thank you to my drill sergeants in the US Army. You put me through the hardest thing I had ever done in my life. It was everything it was supposed to be and more. Nothing that came later would have been possible without having chosen the military.

Thank you to all my counterparts at Badger Challenge. I loved that experience and all of you. It was extraordinarily rewarding. What a remarkable way to spend our summers. It gave me my first opportunity to stand in front of a real audience and deliver an inspirational speech. Without the military, there would have been no Badger Challenge, and without BC there probably would have been no business school.

Thank you, Andy Gronik. You gave me my first professional job. You said yes to me when no one else did. That made all the difference. I learned so much from you about observation, problem-solving, what it looks like to lead, and what it looks like to care deeply. Thank you for your continued friendship and for taking the time to listen.

Thank you, Henry DePew. You have been bigger than life since the first hour I met you. You're fearless, funny, kind, interested, interesting, a connector, and an includer. You're a good human.

Thank you, Rick Zimmerman. You taught me a critical skill I've never forgotten—how to give tough feedback in a way that is clear and calm. Thank you for giving me the chance to earn a full-time job at P&G. Without that chance, I wouldn't be where I am today. It made a difference.

Thank you to all my counterparts at Coors, especially Pat Edson, Laura Sankey, Lee Buxton, and Scott Coors. Pat, clearly this book and what I do today would not have been possible without the innovation work you led at Coors. I didn't know you all that well when we worked together, but your work has changed my life. Thank you for creating the innovations so I could be part of rolling them out. Laura, thank you for the most memorable interview I've ever had. I don't know why, but I have a feeling you were the reason I got the job at Coors. Lee, you never know what you're going to say that inspires someone to think differently and sticks with them years later. Thank you for that. Scott, thanks for being a great counterpart on our Coors Original adventures.

Thank you, Mike Dilbeck, for being my first friend in the National Speakers Association. I finally figured out how to describe what I talk about.

Thank you, Jessica Pettitt, Thom Singer, and Eliz Greene, my mastermind group Batsignal. You are my speaker family and my life family. I'm so thankful for what we have become for one another. What we need when we need it. It's perfect. It's one of those things in life that I could never have anticipated. I appreciate you.

Thank you to all the speakers who helped me get started, made me better, encouraged me, and have become my friends. There are simply too many to list. You know who you are.

Thank you, Stacey Crowley. You have challenged me to take the Because Workshop to the next level. Your ideas, perspective, and support are appreciated by me and valuable to everyone who uses the Framework.

Thank you, Caswell Huff. You were the first client who really believed in me as a speaker, and your support has made a difference. A big one.

Thank you, Johnny Green. You have had unwavering belief in me and what I do. Your belief and advocacy are appreciated.

Thank you, Simon Sinek and Donald Miller. I don't know you, but your work has inspired me to elevate mine. It's not a competition, but I think mine beats yours. Just saying.

# Appendix
## Because Case Study Summary

THE MATRIX that follows includes a summary of every Because example in the book with a categorization of the type of Because they're using.

| Page | Company | Insights | Because | Type |
|------|---------|----------|---------|------|
| 18 | Mohamed Gungu | Locally made, packable, unique, interesting, an experience, a story. | Handmade. He taught me how to make the music of Africa and I can teach others. | Visual Proof. Product Differentiators. |
| 21 | Amazon | Certainty, communication, ease of doing business. | Reviews, ongoing updates, click and we'll take care of the rest. | Social Proof. Proprietary Process. |
| 27 | 6th Avenue Auto | Don't want to pay to go to dealership. | Specialized in Volkswagens. | Specialization. |
| 37 | Netflix | Late fees, movies out of stock, driving to the store. | No late fees, unlimited stock, DVDs in the mail/streaming. | Novel Approach. |
| 46 | Schomp BMW | Haggling on price, takes forever, have to deal with many people. | One price, one person, one hour. | Novel Approach. Product and Service Differentiators. |
| 47 | Angelle Materials | Pouring concrete is stressful, drivers are scary. | We make your day stress-free through communication and execution. | Extra Value. |

| Page | Company | Insights | Because | Type |
|------|---------|----------|---------|------|
| 51 | Caterpillar | Performance, reliability, operating costs. | Hydraulic hybrid. | Innovation. |
| 61 | Domino's Pizza | Pizza tastes bad. | We listened. We changed our recipe. | Unique Ingredients. Proprietary Process. |
| 69 | Papa Johns | Want better pizza. | Better ingredients. | Unique Ingredients. |
| 70 | *Paranormal Activity* | Want to be scared. | People in the audience are scared. | Social Proof. |
| 71 | Plumber | Customers don't like the "window." | We show up at a specific time. | Novel Approach. |
| 81 | Coors Light | Want cold, refreshing beer. | Frost Brew Liner, Cooler Box, Super Cold Draft, color-change label. | Product Differentiators. |
| 92 | WeatherTech | Generic floor mats don't protect my car. | Laser-measured mats. | Quality Substantiation. |

| Page | Company | Insights | Because | Type |
|------|---------|----------|---------|------|
| 100 | LINX | AV installations are an inefficient mess. | LINX tests and kits all installations offsite. | Novel Approach. |
| 103 | Critical Start | Security analysts are overwhelmed by alerts. | Resolves 99.96 percent of security events, elevating the truly critical events to their clients in real time. | Proprietary Technology. |
| 105 | Ivory | Purity is important. | $99\,^{44}/_{100}$ percent pure. So pure it floats. | Statistics. Unique Ingredients. |
| 105 | Dove | Soap dries my skin. | One-quarter moisturizing cream. | Statistics. Unique Ingredients. |
| 106 | Kop-Coat | Glyphosate is not effective anymore. | Kills two hundred weeds glyphosate alone can't kill with one-eighth the application volume. | Unique Formulation. |
| 110 | Rendina Healthcare Real Estate | Want more expertise and speed for less cost. | Specialized in healthcare. Only one who has built for Cleveland Clinic. | Specialization. |

| Page | Company | Insights | Because | Type |
|------|---------|----------|---------|------|
| 115 | Gerry O'Brion, professional speaker | Want speaker to be good on stage and deliver value to the audience. | "Gerry scored 4.9 out of 5 in front of our audience of over nine hundred CEOs and executives." | Social Proof. |
| 117 | Appliance Direct | I want my dishes to be clean. | There was no cake left in the dishwasher when the cycle was done. | Visual Proof. |
| 118 | R&D Leverage | Want to eliminate heat transfer. | Seventeen patents, first blow mold innovations since the '50s. | Innovation. Product Differentiators. Visual Proof. |
| 120 | Grey Goose | Want to drink the best vodka. | "Rated the #1 tasting vodka in the world by the Beverage Testing Institute." | Third-Party Credibility. |
| 120 | J.D. Power | Want unbiased rankings. | Two hundred fully independent benchmarking studies per year. | Third-Party Credibility. |

| Page | Company | Insights | Because | Type |
|---|---|---|---|---|
| 123 | Mercedes | Wiper blades don't last long. | 800,000 more wiping cycles. | Product Differentiators. |
| 126 | Hanover Research | Need a lot of research on a small budget. | Unlimited research for a fixed annual price. | Pricing Structure. |
| 127 | Red Robin | Want burgers at different price points. | Burgers from $6.99 to $15. | Pricing Structure. |
| 128 | Millstone Coffee | Want flavor to match my palate. | Beans combined to match your preferences. | Customization. Proprietary Technology. |
| 128 | Which Wich | Want sandwich made just for me. | Every sandwich can be customized using unique ordering system. | Customization. |
| 129 | Auto parts retailer | Want my parts fast. | Dedicated truck and driver. | Extra Value. |
| 130 | Roofing company | Want good value and for roof to last. | Top-quality shingles for the mid-tier price. | Extra Value. |

| Page | Company | Insights | Because | Type |
|------|---------|----------|---------|------|
| 131 | Ciancio Ciancio Brown | Want to win my legal case. | Collaborate across practice areas. | Company Structure. |
| 132 | Midas | Want my muffler to last. | Guaranteed for as long as you own your car. | Guarantee. |
| 132 | LifeLock | Want protection if my identity is stolen. | Up to $1 million in legal fees. | Guarantee. |
| 133 | Toro | Lawn mowers are hard to start. | Guaranteed to start. | Guarantee. |
| 134 | Dropps | Want clean laundry for a good price, eco-friendly. | Recyclable packaging, no water, six ingredients, many more. | Innovation. Product Differentiators. |
| 139 | Netflix | Don't like TV commercials or waiting to watch episodes. | No commercials, all episodes in a season launched at the same time. | Novel Approach. Innovation. |

| Page | Company | Insights | Because | Type |
|---|---|---|---|---|
| 144 | Kaivac | Restroom cleaning companies have high turnover and quality challenges. | No-touch system cleans sixty times better in one-third of the time. Saves 90 percent of the chemicals and improves employee morale. | Proprietary Technology. Novel Approach. Innovation. |
| 148 | Morton Salt | Salt gets clumpy in humidity. | Anticaking agent, moisture resistant container. | Innovation. |
| 169 | La Bamba | Want a lot of food for a good price. | Burritos as big as your head. | Product Differentiators. |

# Notes

### Why Would I Buy from You?
1. Daniel Kahneman, *Thinking, Fast and Slow* (New York: Farrar, Straus and Giroux, 2011).

### Step 1: Who Is Your Ideal Customer?
1. Coors Brewing Company proprietary research.

### Step 2: What Are Your Insights?
1. Interview with Allen Klose, November 2015.
2. Blockbuster Inc. 2004 Form 10-K, sec.gov/Archives/edgar/data/1085734/000119312505063510/d10k.htm.
3. Blockbuster Inc. 2004 Form 10-K.
4. "Blockbuster Reinstates Late Fees on Video Rentals," *Dallas Morning News*, March 3, 2010, dallasnews.com/business/2010/03/03/blockbuster-reinstates-late-fees-on-video-rentals.
5. Mary Ellen Cagnassola and Lauren Giella, "Fact Check: Did Blockbuster Turn Down Chance to Buy Netflix for $50 Million?" *Newsweek*, March 11, 2021, newsweek.com/fact-check-did-blockbuster-turn-down-chance-buy-netflix-50-million-1575557.
6. Amos Tversky and Daniel Kahneman, "Prospect Theory: An Analysis of Decision Making under Risk." *Econometrica* 47, no. 2 (March 1979): 263–92, doi.org/10.2307/1914185.

### Step 3: What Is Your Outcome?

1. "No One Wants a Drill. What They Want Is the Hole," Quote Investigator, March 23, 2019, quoteinvestigator.com/2019/03/23/drill; Clayton Christensen, Scott Cook, and Taddy Hall, "Marketing Malpractice: The Cause and the Cure," *Harvard Business Review*, December 2005, hbr.org/2005/12/marketing-malpractice-the-cause-and-the-cure.
2. *Pizza Hut, Inc. v. Papa Johns International, Inc.*, 227 F.3d 489 (5th Cir. 2000), Opinion No. 00-10071, September 19, 2000.
3. "Box Office History for *Paranormal Activity* Movies," The Numbers, the-numbers.com/movies/franchise/Paranormal-Activity.

### Step 4: What Is Your Because?

1. Alvin Powell, "Ellen Langer's State of Mindfulness," *Harvard Gazette*, October 1, 2018, news.harvard.edu/gazette/story/2018/10/ellen-langer-talks-mindfulness-health.
2. Robert Cialdini, *Influence: The Psychology of Persuasion* (New York: Harper Collins, 1984).
3. Coors Brewing Company proprietary research.
4. Simon Sinek, *Start with Why: How Great Leaders Inspire Everyone to Take Action* (New York: Penguin, 2009).
5. Bruce Turkel, *All about Them: Grow Your Business by Focusing on Others* (Boston: Da Capo, 2016).

### Proof Type 1: Systematic Proof

1. "2006–2007 Pesticide Market Estimates: Usage (Page 2)—Pesticides—US EPA," United States Environmental Protection Agency, February 18, 2011, archived at web.archive.org/web/20150626092432/https://www.epa.gov/opp00001/pestsales/07pestsales/usage2007_2.htm#3_6.
2. John Peterson Myers et al., "Concerns over Use of Glyphosate-Based Herbicides and Risks Associated with Exposures: A Consensus Statement," *Environmental Health* 15 (February 2016): 19, doi.org/10.1186/s12940-016-0117-0.

### Proof Type 2: Perceived Proof

1. Michael Anderson and Jeremy Magruder, "Learning from the Crowd: Regression Discontinuity Estimates of the Effects of an Online Review Database," *Economic Journal* 122, no. 563 (September 2012): 957–89, doi.org/10.1111/j.1468-0297.2012.02512.x.

2. Christopher Lawton, "Stolichnaya Maker Takes Shot at Dated Ads for Grey Goose," *Wall Street Journal*, April 15, 2005, wsj.com/articles/SB111353566423207920.

3. "About," Beverage Testing Institute, bevtest.com/about.

4. "About Us," J.D. Power, jdpower.com/business/about-us.

5. "History," J.D. Power, jdpower.com/business/about-us-history.

### Proof Type 3: Created Proof

1. "Midas, Inc.," Dun & Bradstreet, dnb.com/business-directory/company-profiles.midas_inc.3c25b0cb3aa4ebd9e2880fd17c70486d.html.

2. "Our Midas Guarantees," Midas, midas.com/about-midas/our-midas-guarantees.

### Step 5: Innovate

1. Sandvine, *Global Internet Phenomena: Latin America and North America*, May 2015, sandvine.com/hubfs/Sandvine_Redesign_2019/Downloads/Internet%20Phenomena/2015-global-internet-phenomena-report-latin-america-and-north-america.pdf.

### Step 7: Execute at Every Touchpoint

1. "Tiger Woods," PGA Tournament, pgatour.com/players/player.08793.tiger-woods.html.

2. Kahneman, *Thinking, Fast and Slow*.

PHOTO: JOHN DEMATO

# About the Author

GERRY O'BRION is a speaker, author, and creator of the Because Framework of Influence. The Framework has helped over fifty thousand CEOs, business owners, and sales teams stand out from the sea of sameness and grow their sales.

Gerry began his career in marketing at Procter & Gamble and then was an executive for Coors Light, Quiznos, and Red Robin. He has his MBA from the University of Michigan.

He spent eight years serving in the military.

He lives in Greenwood Village, Colorado, along with four goats, five ducks, twelve chickens, two hives of bees, and several wild bunnies.

Made in United States
Orlando, FL
29 April 2024

46322503R00136